200
FAMILY-FAVORED
HOME PLANS

Move-Up Designs From 2400 To 4000 Square Feet

HOME PLANNERS, INC.
Tucson, Arizona

Published by Home Planners, Inc.
Editorial and Corporate Offices:
3275 West Ina Road, Suite 110
Tucson, Arizona 85741

Distribution Center:
29333 Lorie Lane
Wixom, Michigan 48393

Rickard D. Bailey, President and Publisher
Cindy J. Coatsworth, Publications Manager
Paulette Mulvin, Senior Editor
Beth Nickey, Project Editor
Paul D. Fitzgerald, Book Designer

Photo Credits
Front Cover: © Susan Miller
Back Cover: © Dave Dawson Photography

First Printing, September 1993
10   9   8   7   6   5   4   3   2   1

Printed in the United States of America.

ISBN softcover: 1-881955-07-9
ISBN hardback: 1-881955-11-7

On the front cover: Design Z9822, page 35.
On the back cover: Design Z9812, page 133; Design Z9871, page 122.

TABLE OF CONTENTS

EDITOR'S NOTE

As families grow and lifestyles change, the once-cozy first home may begin to feel cramped. This unique collection of homes offers a variety of plans geared toward the family ready to move up to a home with room for everyone. Key design features include multiple bedrooms, including luxurious master suites; separate formal and informal living areas; amenity-filled kitchens and bonus rooms. A large assortment of exterior styles and livable floor plans insures that this book offers just the right plan for you and your family.

About The Designers

The Blue Ribbon Designer Series™ is a collection of books featuring the home plans of a diverse group of outstanding home designers and architects known as the Blue Ribbon Network of Designers. This group of companies is dedicated to creating and marketing the finest possible plans for home construction on a regional and national basis. Each of the companies exhibits superior work and integrity in all phases of the stock-plan business including modern, trendsetting floor planning, a professionally executed blueprint package and a strong sense of service and commitment to the consumer.

Design Basics, Inc.

For nearly a decade, Design Basics, a nationally recognized home design service located in Omaha, has been developing plans for custom home builders. Since 1987, the firm has consistently appeared in *Builder* magazine, the official magazine of the National Association of Home Builders, as the top-selling designer. The company's plans also regularly appear in numerous other shelter magazines such as *Better Homes and Gardens*, *House Beautiful* and *Home Planner*.

Design Traditions

Design Traditions was established by Stephen S. Fuller with the tenets of innovation, quality, originality and uncompromising architectural techniques in traditional and European homes. Especially popular throughout the Southeast, Design Traditions' plans are known for their extensive detail and thoughtful design. They are widely published in such shelter magazines as *Southern Living* magazine and *Better Homes and Gardens*.

Alan Mascord Design Associates, Inc.

Founded in 1983 as a local supplier to the building community, Mascord Design Associates of Portland, Oregon, began to successfully publish plans nationally in 1985. With plans now drawn exclusively on computer, Mascord Design Associates quickly received a reputation for homes that are easy to build yet meet the rigorous demands of the buyers' market, winning local and national awards. The company's trademark is creating floor plans that work well and exhibit excellent traffic patterns. Their motto is: "Drawn to build, designed to sell."

Larry W. Garnett & Associates, Inc.

Starting as a designer of homes for Houston-area residents, Garnett & Associates has been marketing designs nationally for the past ten years. A well-respected design firm, the company's plans are regularly featured in *House Beautiful*, *Country Living*, *Home* and *Professional Builder*. Numerous accolades, including several from the Texas Institute of Building Design and the American Institute of Building Design, have been awarded to the company for excellence in architecture.

Home Planners, Inc.

Headquartered in Tucson, Arizona, with additional offices in Detroit, Home Planners is one of the longest-running and most successful home design firms in the United States. With over 2,500 designs in its portfolio, the company provides a wide range of styles, sizes and types of homes for the residential builder. All of Home Planners' designs are created with the care and professional expertise that fifty years of experience in the home-planning business affords. Their homes are designed to be built, lived in and enjoyed for years to come.

Donald A. Gardner, Architect, Inc.

The South Carolina firm of Donald A. Gardner was established in response to a growing demand for residential designs that reflect constantly changing lifestyles. The company's specialty is providing homes with refined, custom-style details and unique features such as passive-solar designs and open floor plans. Computer-aided design and drafting technology resulting in trouble-free construction documents places the firm at the leading edge of the home plan industry.

Home Design Services, Inc.

For the past fifteen years, Home Design Services of Longwood, Florida, has been formulating plans for the sun-country lifestyle. At the forefront of design innovation and imagination, the company has developed award-winning designs that are consistently praised for their highly detailed, free-flowing floor plans, imaginative and exciting interior architecture and elevations which have gained international appeal.

Colonial Home Plans

The first American housing style was based on building techniques colonists brought over from England. Early Colonial style is a straightforward, time-tested design. Colonial homes were constructed with a good sense of proportion and shaped like small boxes, with simple, rectangular floor plans inside.

Colonial houses were one or two stories high and usually only one room deep. They had steeply pitched gable or gambrel roofs covered with wood shingles. The post-and-beam construction of early settlers has been replaced in larger homes by platform frames.

Popular characteristics of Colonial homes included large central or end chimneys with decorative tops, tiny windows with diamond-shaped panes, board-and-batten doors, and wood or brick exterior walls. An overhanging second story, or jetty, was borrowed from Medieval building traditions.

Expanding from the basic box, builders discovered an easy way to add space by constructing a simple lean-to across the rear of the lower story. This extra room was used for the kitchen and storage space or an additional bedroom. This sloping Colonial house was described as a Saltbox, or, in the South, a catslide.

The designs on the following pages have come a long way from the basic box. Larger, more complex floor plans, varied building materials and architecturally interesting facades are accompanied by the same sense of simple, practical style that distinguishes Colonial homes.

Design by
Home Planners,
Inc.

Design Z3563

First Floor: 1,023 square feet
Second Floor: 886 square feet
Total: 1,889 square feet

● Practical to build, this wonderful transitional plan combines the best of contemporary and traditional styling. Its stucco exterior is enhanced by arched windows and a recessed arched entry plus a lovely balcony off the second-floor master bedroom. A walled entry court extends the living room on the outside. The double front doors open to a foyer with hall closet and powder room. The service entrance is just to the right and accesses the two-car garage. The large living room adjoins directly to the dining room. The family room is set off behind the garage and features a sloped ceiling and fireplace. Sleeping quarters consist of two secondary bedrooms with a shared bath and a generous master suite with well-appointed bath.

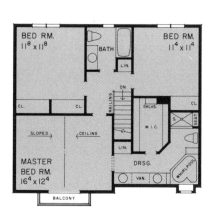

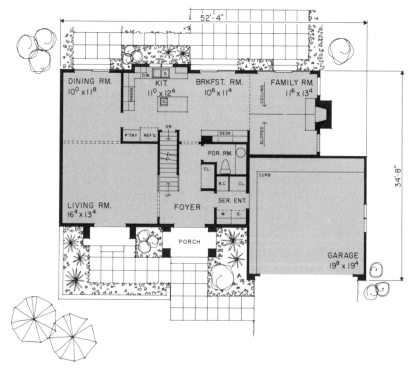

Design Z3550

First Floor: 2,328 square feet
Second Floor: 712 square feet
Total: 3,040 square feet

● A transitional 1½-story home combines the best of contemporary and traditional elements. This one uses vertical wood siding, stone and multi-paned windows to beautiful advantage. The floor plan makes great use of space with first-floor living and dining areas and a first-floor master suite. Two secondary bedrooms, a full bath and an open lounge area are found on the second floor. The garage is accessed from the island kitchen through the laundry.

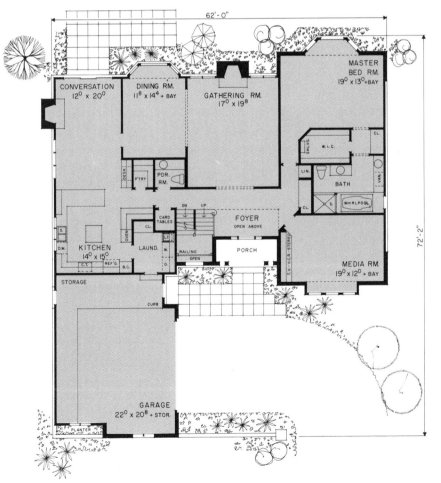

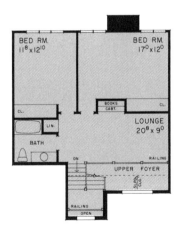

Design by
Home Planners,
Inc.

Design Z3334

First Floor: 2,193 square feet
Second Floor: 831 square feet
Total: 3,024 square feet

● A traditional favorite, this home combines classic style with progressive floor planning. Four bedrooms are split — master suite and one bedroom on the first floor, two more bedrooms upstairs. The second-floor lounge overlooks a large, sunken gathering room near the formal dining area. A handy butler's pantry connects the dining room and kitchen.

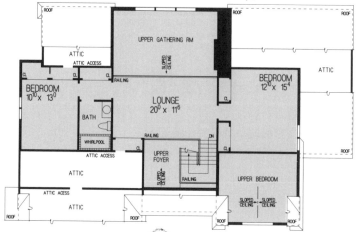

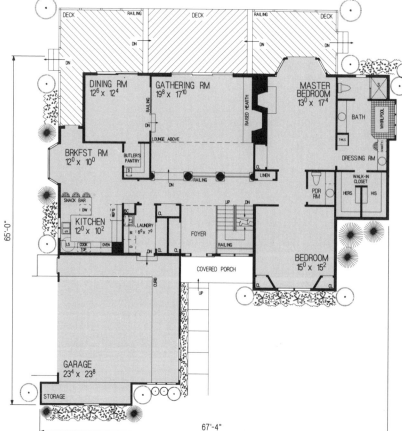

Design by
Home Planners,
Inc.

● One of the most popular home renditions is the two-story four-bedroom, and few designs of this type offer as much as the one shown here. The gracious entry opens to the right to a media room and to a living room with fireplace. On the left is a formal dining room. At the back, find the kitchen with attached breakfast room and just a step down is everyone's favorite family room. All four bedrooms are located on the second floor. The master suite features a double-size walk-in closet and bumped-out window in the bath. Three family bedrooms share a full bath.

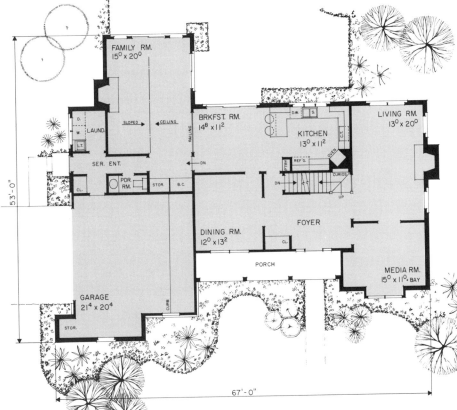

Design Z3365

First Floor: 1,731 square feet
Second Floor: 1,248 square feet
Total: 2,979 square feet

Design by
Home Planners,
Inc.

Design Z2995

First Floor: 2,465 square feet
Second Floor: 617 square feet
Total: 3,082 square feet

● This New England Colonial delivers beautiful proportions and great livability on 1½ levels. The main area of the house, the first floor, holds a living room, library, family room, dining room and gourmet kitchen. The master bedroom, also on this floor, features a whirlpool tub and sloped ceiling. A long rear terrace stretches the full width of the house. Two bedrooms on the second floor share a full bath; each has a built-in desk.

Design by
Home Planners,
Inc.

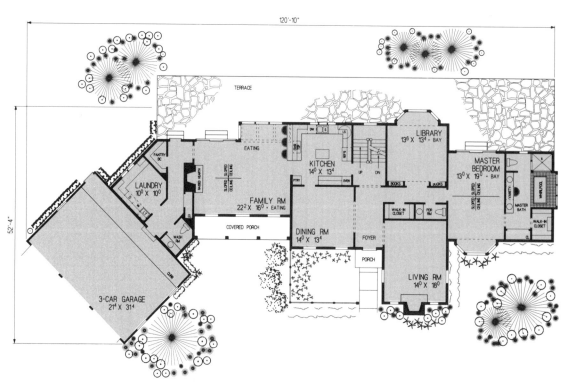

Design by
**Home Planners,
Inc.**

● The exterior detailing of this design recalls 18th-Century New England architecture. Enter by way of the centered front door and you are greeted into the foyer. Directly to the right is the study or optional bedroom or to the left is the living room. This large formal room features sliding glass doors to the sundrenched solarium. The beauty of the solarium will be appreciated from the master bedroom and the dining room along with the living room.

Design Z2615
First Floor: 2,563 square feet
Second Floor: 552 square feet
Total: 3,115 square feet

Design by
Home Planners,
Inc.

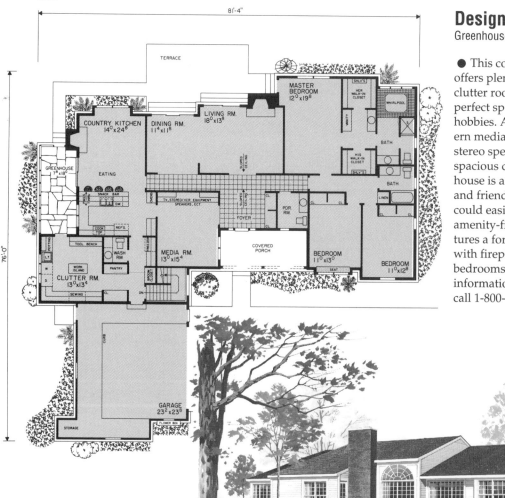

Design Z2880 Living Area: 2,758 square feet
Greenhouse: 149 square feet; Total: 2,907 square feet

● This comfortable traditional home offers plenty of modern livability. A clutter room off the two-car garage is the perfect space for workbench, sewing or hobbies. Across the hall one finds a modern media room, the perfect place for stereo speakers, videos and more. A spacious country kitchen off the greenhouse is a cozy gathering place for family and friends. The 149-foot greenhouse itself could easily be the focal point of this amenity-filled home. The house also features a formal dining room, living room with fireplace, covered porch, and three bedrooms including a master suite. For information on customizing this design, call 1-800-322-6797, ext. 800.

Design Z2888
Square Footage: 3,018

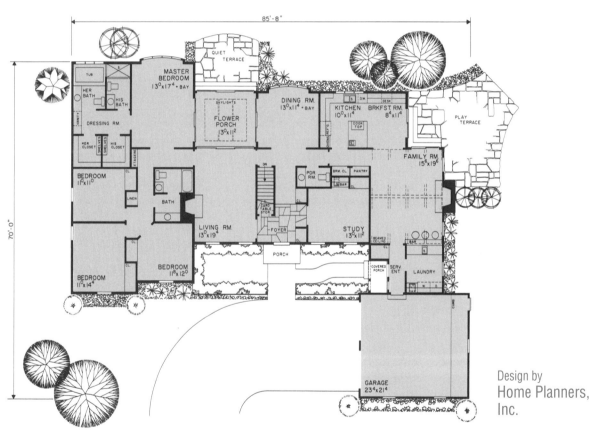

Design by
Home Planners,
Inc.

● This is an outstanding Early American design for the 20th-Century. The exterior detailing with narrow clapboards, multi-paned windows and cupola are the features of yesteryear. Interior planning, though, is for today's active family. Formal living room, in-formal family room plus a study are present. Every activity will have its place in this home. Picture yourself working in the kitchen. There's enough counter space for two or three helpers. Four bedrooms are in the private area. Stop and imagine your daily routine if you occupied the master bedroom. Both you and your spouse would have plenty of space and privacy. The flower porch, accessible from the master bedroom, living and dining rooms, is a very delightful "plus" feature. Study this design's every detail.

Design Z9823

First Floor: 1,960 square feet
Second Floor: 905 square feet
Total: 2,865 square feet

● The classical styling of this Colonial home will be appreciated by traditionalists. The foyer opens to both a banquet-sized dining room and formal living room with fireplace. Just beyond, is the two-story great room. The entire right side of the main level is taken up by the master suite.

The other side of the main level includes a large kitchen and breakfast room just steps away from the detached garage. Upstairs, each bedroom features ample closet space and direct access to bathrooms. The detached garage features an unfinished office or studio on its second level.

WIDTH 69'-5"
DEPTH 74'-6"

Design by
Design Traditions

Design Z9865

First Floor: 1,495 square feet
Second Floor: 1,600 square feet
Total: 3,095 square feet

● Complete with widow's walk detailing and pedimented front entry, this wood-and-stone cottage is a true delight. Formal living and dining dominate the right side of the plan while more casual gathering and eating areas are found to the rear. The second floor holds a master suite with sitting room and exercise room in addition to three family bedrooms.

Design by
Design Traditions

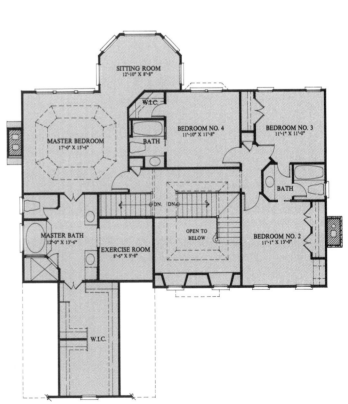

DECK

BREAKFAST
12'-10" X 10'-0"

KITCHEN
16'-0" X 15'-6"

FAMILY ROOM
19'-0" X 15'-6"

DINING ROOM
13'-0" X 14'-2"

UP

DN

LAUNDRY

POWDER

TWO STORY
FOYER
13'-10" X 12'-6"

UP

LIVING ROOM
13'-0" X 13'-6"

STOOP

TWO CAR GARAGE
20'-10" X 21'-4"

WIDTH 49'
DEPTH 57'

SITTING ROOM
12'-10" X 8'-8"

W.I.C.

MASTER BEDROOM
17'-0" X 15'-6"

BATH

BEDROOM NO. 4
11'-10" X 11'-8"

BEDROOM NO. 3
11'-1" X 11'-0"

BATH

MASTER BATH
12'-0" X 13'-6"

DN. DN.

EXERCISE ROOM
8'-6" X 9'-8"

OPEN TO
BELOW

BEDROOM NO. 2
11'-1" X 13'-0"

W.I.C.

Design Z9390

First Floor: 1,865 square feet
Second Floor: 774 square feet
Total: 2,639 square feet

● A magnificent brick facade with a 3-car, side-load garage conceals a well-organized floor plan. A tiled foyer leads to the formal dining room, with wet bar and hutch space, on the left and a parlor on the right. Straight ahead is a spacious great room with arched windows flanking a fireplace. The kitchen offers a snack bar peninsula and adjoins a bayed breakfast area. The first-floor master bedroom includes a large walk-in closet and French doors leading to a master bath with angled whirlpool and shower with glass block. The second floor provides three bedrooms and two full baths. A reading seat flanked by two cabinets overlooks the volume entry.

Design by
Design
Basics,
Inc.

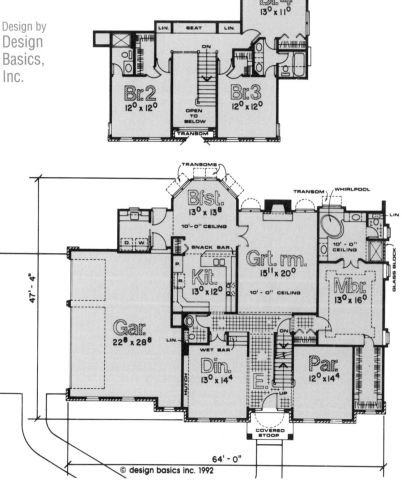

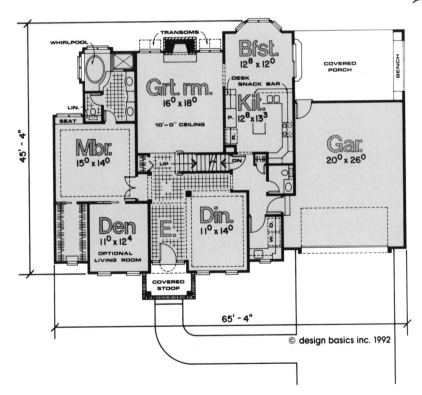

WHIRLPOOL

TRANSOMS

LIN.

SEAT

Grt. rm.
16⁰ x 18⁰

10'-0" CEILING

Bfst.
12⁸ x 12⁰

DESK | SNACK BAR

Kit.
12⁸ x 13³

P.

R.

COVERED PORCH

BENCH

Mbr.
15⁰ x 14⁰

UP

DN

Gar.
20⁰ x 26⁰

Den
11⁰ x 12⁴

OPTIONAL LIVING ROOM

E.

Din.
11⁰ x 14⁰

W/D.

COVERED STOOP

45'- 4"

65'- 4"

© design basics inc. 1992

Design by
**Design
Basics,
Inc.**

Design Z9379

First Floor: 1,716 square feet
Second Floor: 716 square feet
Total: 2,432 square feet

● This Colonial elevation makes a comfortable yet impressive statement. A volume entry opens to the formal dining room defined by special ceiling treatment and flooring materials. The great room with 10-foot ceiling features a fireplace. The kitchen offers a wraparound counter with a Lazy Susan, a large pantry, a planning desk and an island. A sunny breakfast bay features sliding glass doors to a covered porch. The master bedroom includes a pampering master bath with a whirlpool, shower and dual lavatories, a large walk-in closet and access to a private den. Three bedrooms and a full bath occupy the second floor.

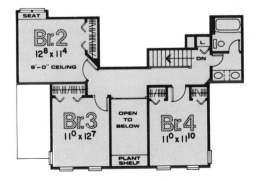

SEAT

Br. 2
12⁸ x 11⁴

9'-0" CEILING

DN

L

Br. 3
11⁰ x 12⁷

OPEN TO BELOW

Br. 4
11⁰ x 11¹⁰

PLANT SHELF

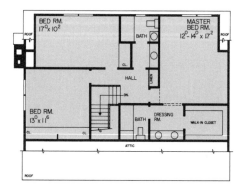

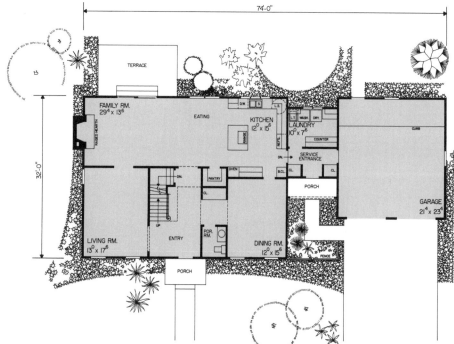

Design by
Home Planners,
Inc.

Design Z2596
First Floor: 1,489 square feet
Second Floor: 982 square feet
Total: 2,471 square feet

● A splendid rendition of Cape Cod styling, this plan is a cozy space to come home to. An L-shaped kitchen with island range, adjacent eating area, and family room that features a raised-hearth fireplace and access to a rear terrace are first-floor highlights. Note, too, the formal dining room, comfy living room, spacious entry, and sheltered service entrance that leads to an extra-large laundry room with additional counter space. Upstairs are big bedrooms, including a master suite with a large, walk-in closet.

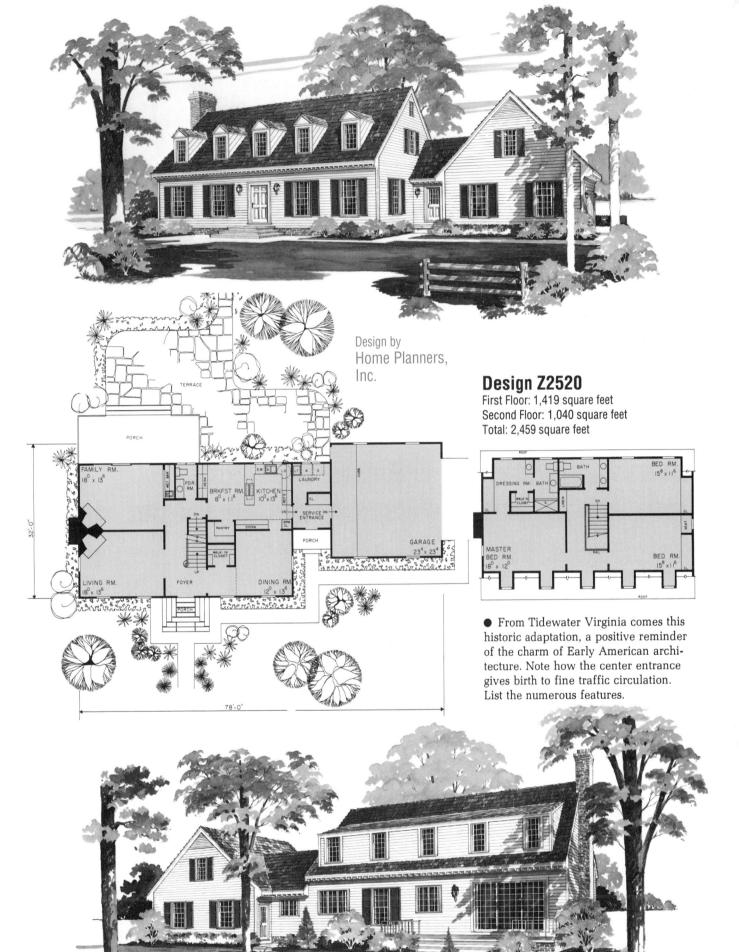

Design by
Home Planners,
Inc.

TERRACE

PORCH

FAMILY RM.
18⁰ x 13⁶

PDR. RM.

BRKFST RM.
8⁰ x 11⁶

KITCHEN
10⁰ x 13⁶

LAUNDRY

SERVICE ENTRANCE

GARAGE
23⁴ x 23⁴

PORCH

PANTRY

CHINA

WALK IN CLOSET

LIVING RM.
18⁰ x 13⁶

FOYER

DINING RM.
12⁰ x 13⁶

PORCH

32'-0"

78'-0"

Design Z2520
First Floor: 1,419 square feet
Second Floor: 1,040 square feet
Total: 2,459 square feet

ROOF

BATH

BED RM.
15⁸ x 11⁶

DRESSING RM.

BATH

LINEN

WALK IN CLOSET

MASTER
BED RM.
18⁰ x 12⁰

BED RM.
15⁸ x 11⁶

ROOF

● From Tidewater Virginia comes this historic adaptation, a positive reminder of the charm of Early American architecture. Note how the center entrance gives birth to fine traffic circulation. List the numerous features.

19

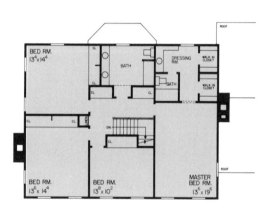

BED RM.
13⁴ x 14⁴

BATH

DRESSING
RM.

WALK-IN
CLOSET

ROOF

CL

BATH

WALK-IN
CLOSET

CL

DN

CL

ROOF

BED RM.
13⁶ x 14⁴

BED RM.
13⁸ x 10²

MASTER
BED RM.
13 x 19⁶

Design by
Home Planners,
Inc.

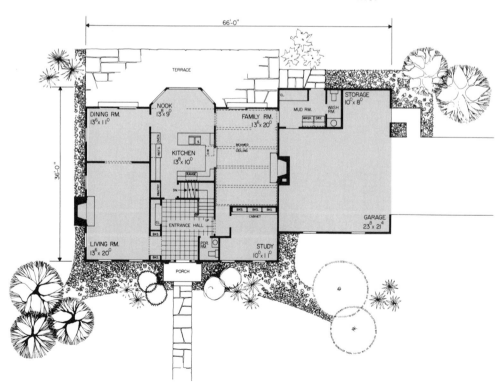

66'-0"

TERRACE

DINING RM.
13⁶ x 11⁰

NOOK
13⁶ x 9

FAMILY RM.
13⁶ x 20⁰

STORAGE
10' x 8⁰

MUD. RM.

WASH
RM.

WASH DRY

36'-0"

KITCHEN
13⁶ x 10⁰

REF'G

OVEN

BEAMED
CEILING

RANGE

PANTRY

DN

BKS.
BKS.
BKS.

CL

BKS.

CABINET

GARAGE
23⁸ x 21⁴

LIVING RM.
13⁶ x 20⁰

ENTRANCE HALL

PDR.
RM.

STUDY
10' x 11⁰

BKS.

PORCH

Design Z2610

First Floor: 1,505 square feet
Second Floor: 1,344 square feet
Total: 2,849 square feet

● This full two-story traditional will be noteworthy wherever built. It strongly recalls images of a New England of yesteryear. And well it might, for the window treatment is delightful. The front entrance detail is inviting. The narrow horizontal siding and the corner boards are appealing as are the two massive chimneys. The center entrance hall is large with a handy powder room nearby. The study has built-in bookshelves and offers a full measure of privacy. The interior kitchen has a pass-through to the family room and enjoys all that natural light from the bay window of the nook. A beamed ceiling, fireplace and sliding glass doors are features of the family room. The mud room highlights a closet, laundry equipment and an extra wash room. Study the upstairs with four bedrooms, two baths and plenty of closets. An excellent arrangement for all.

Design Z2659 First Floor: 1,023 square feet

Second Floor: 1,008 square feet; Third Floor: 476 square feet
Total: 2,507 square feet

● The facade of this three-storied, pitch-roofed house has a symmetrical placement of windows and a restrained but elegant central entrance. The central hall, or foyer, expands midway through the house to a family kitchen. Off the foyer are two rooms, a living room with fireplace and a study. The windowed third floor attic can be used as a study and studio. Three bedrooms are housed on the second floor.

Design by
Home Planners,
Inc.

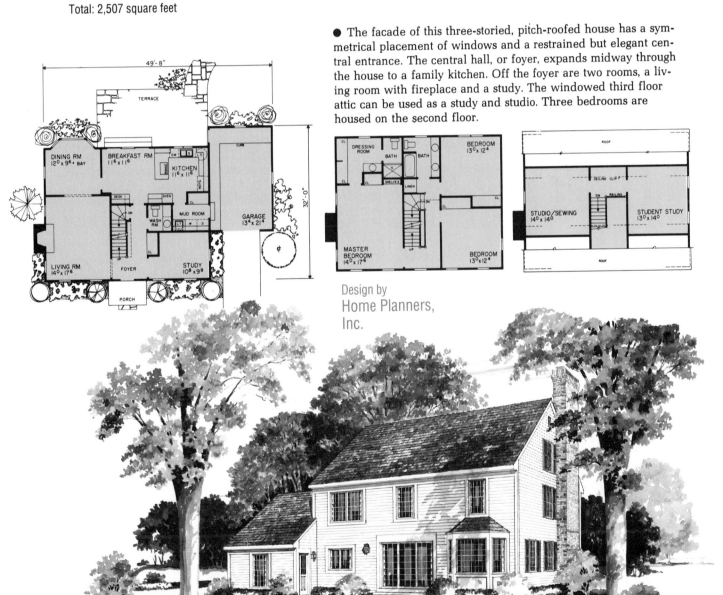

Design Z3366

Main Level: 1,638 square feet
Upper Level: 650 square feet
Lower Level: 934 square feet
Total: 3,222 square feet

● There is much more to this design than meets the eye. While it may look like a 1½-story plan, bonus recreation and hobby space in the walk-out basement adds almost 1,000 square feet. The first floor holds living and dining areas as well as the master bedroom suite. Two family bedrooms on the second floor are connected by a balcony area that overlooks the gathering room below. Notice the covered porch beyond the breakfast and dining rooms.

Design by
Home Planners,
Inc.

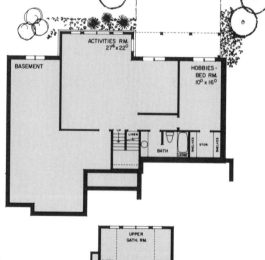

American Traditional Designs

American architecture has developed from early Colonial designs to a distinctive traditional style. American Traditional designs have a classic sense of formality, elegance and style. The elevations are impressive, yet unassuming.

The designs on the following pages are distinguished by brick exteriors with formal entranceways, round-top windows and multi-gabled roofs. Although generally two-story homes, one- or $1^1/_2$-story versions occur. The modern designs included in this section feature attached two- or three-car garages, open living areas, window bays and fireplaces.

Each of the American Traditional home plans has been designed to accommodate a large family. The floor plans include large living areas with many built-ins. Formal and informal areas flow together for ease in entertaining. The sleeping zones are spacious, and many take advantage of nearby game rooms or bonus rooms.

Design Z9085 on page 24 features a three-car, side-load garage which creates a secluded courtyard accessible from the master bedroom. A three-car garage is placed to the rear of Design Z3552 on page 32, which also features a solarium. These unique features and other luxurious amenities such as wet bars and butler's pantries enhance each of the traditional designs in this section.

Design Z9085

First Floor: 2,467 square feet
Second Floor: 710 square feet
Total: 3,177 square feet

Design by
Larry W.
Garnett &
Associates, Inc.

● With dramatic transitional appeal this brick two-story home has a floor plan that is impressive. From the central foyer, go left to a sunken living room with a view of the formal dining room. A gameroom adjoins the U-shaped kitchen with attached breakfast nook. To the right is the master bedroom suite with twelve-foot ceiling and luxury bath. Note the access to the courtyard from this room as well as from the gameroom. Guest quarters lie to the rear of the first-floor plan. A curving staircase to the second floor leads to two additional bedrooms which share a full bath. The upstairs balcony overlooks the foyer below.

Guest Quarters
11' x 13'

Bath 2

3-Car Garage

Breakfast
10' x 10'

French Door

Util.

Kitchen
14' x 13'

Wet Bar

Gameroom
20'-4" x 14'-8"
Volume Clg.

Courtyard

Pantry

French Doors

Dining
13'-4" x 11'-4"

Porch

42" High Wall

French Doors

Foyer

French Doors

Bath
Barrel
Vaulted
Clg.

Sunken
Living Room
17' x 17'-4"
14' Clg.

Master Bedroom
14' x 21'
12' Clg.

Mirrored
Doors

Bedroom 3
16' x 14'

Stor.

Gameroom Below

Bath 3

Bedroom 2
11' x 14'

Foyer Below

WIDTH 55'
DEPTH 78'-8"

9' Clg. Throughout Second Floor

10' Clg. Throughout First Floor
Unless Otherwise Noted

Design Z9112

First Floor: 1,951 square feet
Second Floor: 970 square feet
Total: 2,921 square feet

● A beautiful open living area is the first noticeable item in this home's floor plan. There is the living room on the right with fireplace and the formal dining room on the left connecting to the kitchen with a pocket door. A lovely gallery leads to the glass-enclosed breakfast area and to the master bedroom suite. French doors open to a rear porch. Upstairs there are three bedrooms and a full bath. Each bedroom has a walk-in closet; Bedroom 2 has a built-in desk and cabinets. The two-car garage has a huge work area to the rear.

Design by
Larry W.
Garnett &
Associates, Inc.

WIDTH 82'-8"
DEPTH 64'-4"

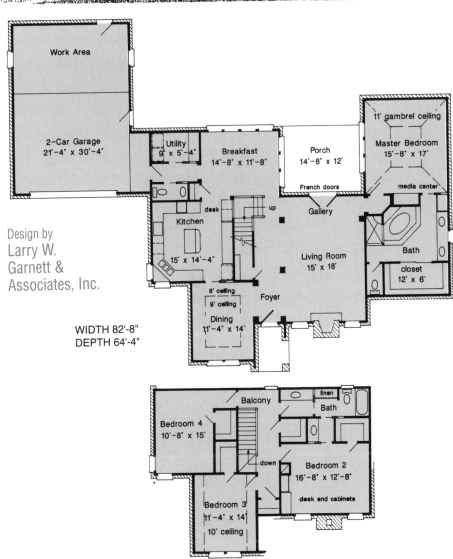

Design by
**Larry W.
Garnett &
Associates, Inc.**

Design Z9029

First Floor: 1,208 square feet
Second Floor: 1,066 square feet
Total: 2,274 square feet

WIDTH 60'
DEPTH 36'-8"

● This quaint little plan works so well on narrow lots that you might never suspect all the livability that can be found inside. From the front foyer turn right to the wonderfully open living room that has as its focus an open hearth through to the rear family room. A left turn from the foyer leads to a formal dining room with bay window. Another bay window can be found in the breakfast room which is next to an efficient L-shaped kitchen. Upstairs are three lovely bedrooms. Be sure to investigate all the features of the master suite: a sitting room, double walk-in closet, and separate tub and shower.

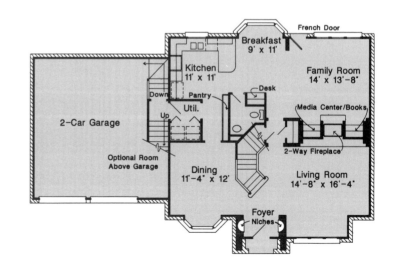

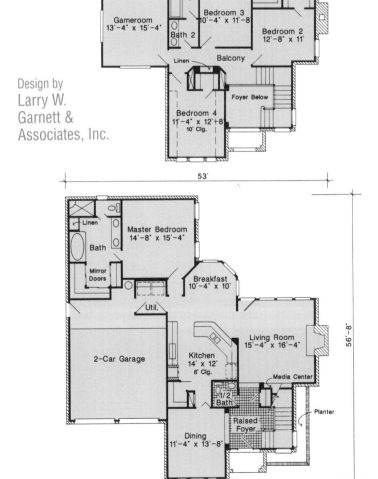

Design by
Larry W.
Garnett &
Associates, Inc.

Gameroom
13'-4" x 15'-4"

Bedroom 3
10'-4" x 11'-8"

Bath 2

Bedroom 2
12'-8" x 11'

Linen

Balcony

Foyer Below

Bedroom 4
11'-4" x 12'+8"
10' Clg.

53'

Linen

Bath

Master Bedroom
14'-8" x 15'-4"

Mirror Doors

Breakfast
10'-4" x 10'

Util.

2-Car Garage

Kitchen
14' x 12'
8' Clg.

Living Room
15'-4" x 16'-4"

Media Center

1/2 Bath

Raised Foyer

Planter

Dining
11'-4" x 13'-8"

56'-8"

Design Z9127

First Floor: 1,565 square feet
Second Floor: 967 square feet
Total: 2,532 square feet

● An impressive plan, rich with detail, this brick home serves the needs of just about any size family. Living and dining areas radiate around the central hub kitchen with attached bay-windowed breakfast area. The master bedroom takes position on the first floor, to the rear of the plan and away from family bedrooms upstairs. Each of these family bedrooms has a walk-in closet and all share a compartmented bath. A game room is situated over the garage and has windows on two walls for plenty of light and refreshing breezes.

27

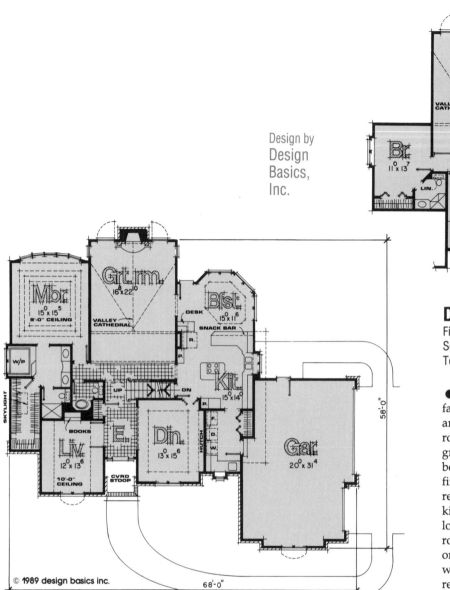

Design by
**Design
Basics,
Inc.**

Design Z9244

First Floor: 1,972 square feet
Second Floor: 893 square feet
Total: 2,865 square feet

● Natural light floods the hard-surfaced entry area of this home—an area flanked by the formal living room and dining room. The massive great room to the rear of the plan boasts a valley cathedral ceiling and fireplace framed by windows to the rear yard. A grand gourmet island kitchen has two pantries and overlooks the gazebo dinette. Split-bedroom planning puts the master suite on the first floor. Besides its bow window and tiered ceiling, this retreat features a whirlpool tub, His and Hers vanities, skylit walk-in closet and compartmented stool and shower. Upstairs bedrooms include two with a Hollywood bath and one with its own three-quarter bath.

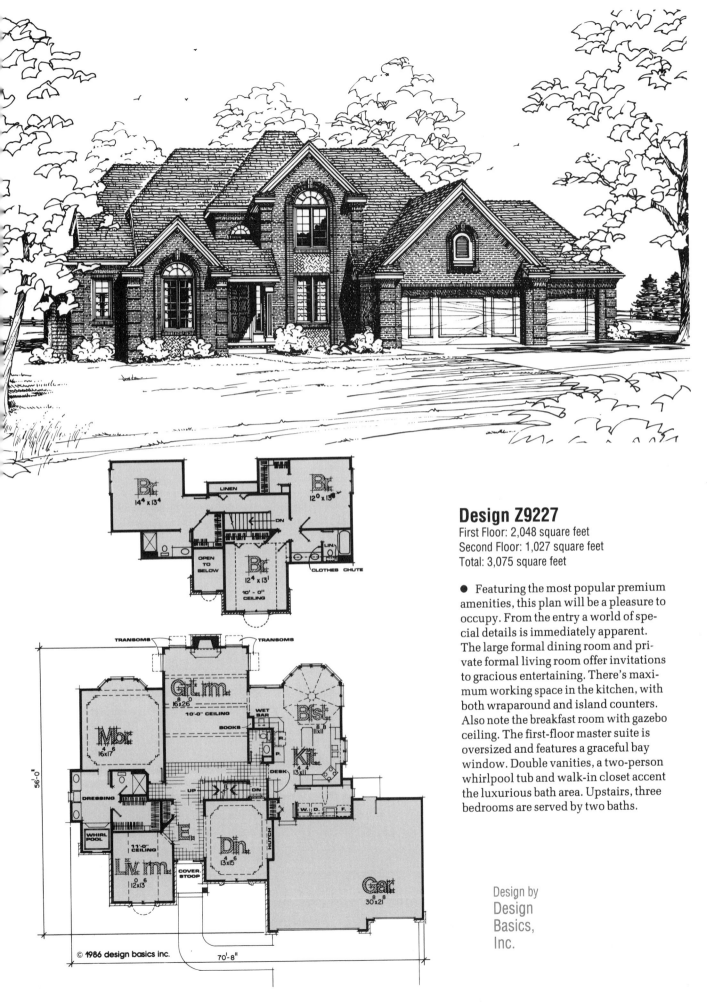

Design Z9227

First Floor: 2,048 square feet
Second Floor: 1,027 square feet
Total: 3,075 square feet

● Featuring the most popular premium amenities, this plan will be a pleasure to occupy. From the entry a world of special details is immediately apparent. The large formal dining room and private formal living room offer invitations to gracious entertaining. There's maximum working space in the kitchen, with both wraparound and island counters. Also note the breakfast room with gazebo ceiling. The first-floor master suite is oversized and features a graceful bay window. Double vanities, a two-person whirlpool tub and walk-in closet accent the luxurious bath area. Upstairs, three bedrooms are served by two baths.

Design by
Design
Basics,
Inc.

Design Z9279 First Floor: 2,078 square feet; Second Floor: 960 square feet; Total: 3,038 square feet

● Custom touches adorn the elevation of this luxurious four-bedroom, 1½-story home. Inside, the two-story high entry has clear views of the sunken great room. This area features a fireplace, sloped ceiling and built-in entertainment center. Just off the entry, French doors access a private library while the formal dining room contains a hutch space and benefits from a wet bar/servery. Families will appreciate the gourmet kitchen with island counter, walk-in pantry and planning desk. At the end of the day, retreat to the master suite with built-in bookcases, a double vanity, walk-in closet and two-person whirlpool tub. Upstairs, the open entry leads to three generous secondary bedrooms.

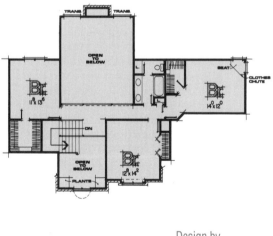

Design by
Design
Basics,
Inc.

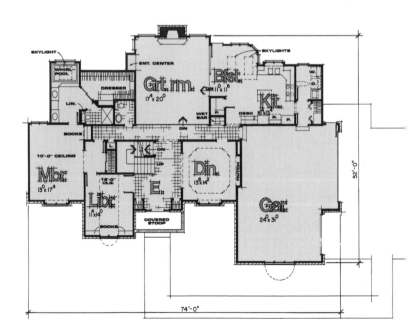

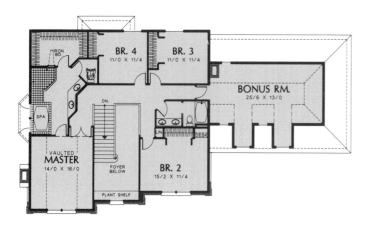

◀ 74' ▶

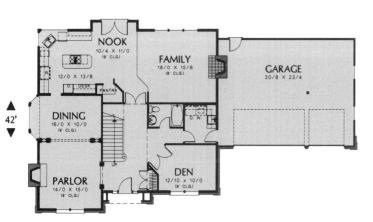

▲
42'
▼

Design Z9511

First Floor: 1,575 square feet
Second Floor: 1,329 square feet
Total: 2,904 square feet
Bonus Room: 424 square feet

● This elegant four-bedroom home easily accommodates the large family. A stately brick facade with twin chimneys greets visitors. A covered entryway leads to a two-story foyer with coat closet and plant shelf. A formal parlor with a fireplace is to the left, adjacent to the formal dining room with bay window. The kitchen provides an island cooktop, planning desk, pantry and breakfast nook. A second fireplace is located in the family room. With a full bath located on the first floor, the den can alternate as a guest room. The second floor offers four bedrooms and a large bonus room. The master bedroom with vaulted ceiling includes a luxurious bath with spa tub, dual vanities and a walk-in closet with a built-in ironing board.

Design by
Alan Mascord
Design Associates, Inc.

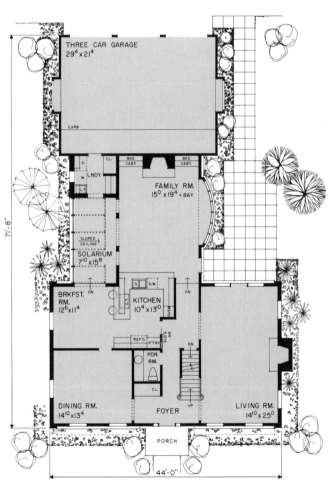

Design Z3552

First Floor: 1,784 square feet
Second Floor: 1,192 square feet
Total: 2,976 square feet

● Smart exterior features mark this home as a classic: second-story pop-outs with half-round windows above multi-paned windows, charming lintels and a combination of horizontal wood siding and brick. Its interior floor plan contains both formal and informal areas, two fireplaces, a cozy solarium and three bedrooms with a sitting room. A three-car garage provides all the space necessary for the family vehicles and additional paraphernalia.

Design by
Home Planners,
Inc.

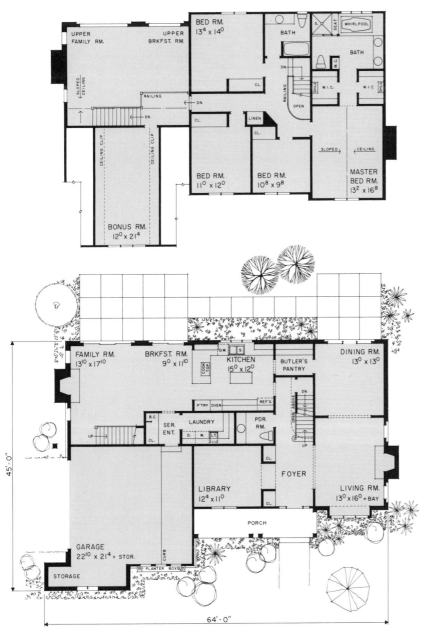

Design Z3551

First Floor: 1,575 square feet
Second Floor: 1,501 square feet
Total: 3,076 square feet

● Efficient floor planning provides a spacious, yet economical home. The large kitchen adjoins a breakfast/family room combination with fireplace. A butler's pantry connects the kitchen to the formal dining room with terrace access. A second fireplace is found in the living room. Also on the first floor: a library and convenient powder room. The master bedroom features His and Hers walk-in closets and a grand bath with whirlpool tub. The bedroom next door would make a fine nursury or office. A large bonus room over the garage offers many optional uses.

Design by
Home Planners,
Inc.

R.DENT

great room are the spacious kitchen and bayed breakfast area. A back staircase is included for easy access to upstairs bedrooms. The second floor provides three bedrooms with various bath combinations. A balcony provides a breathtaking view of the great room and foyer below. The master suite features a tray ceiling and sitting area warmed by sunlight from an angled window combination. The enormous master bath area includes a tray ceiling and His and Hers vanities and closets.

WIDTH 63'-10"
DEPTH 48'-6"

Design by
Design Traditions

Design Z9913
First Floor: 1,625 square feet
Second Floor: 1,750 square feet
Total: 3,375 square feet

WIDTH 63'-10"
DEPTH 48'-6"

● This American Country home, with its clapboard siding, covered balcony and shuttered windows, echoes images of traditional small-town living. The two-story foyer serves as an entrance into traditional, classical styling. Opening to the foyer are the din-[ing room] and formal living room. The two-[story gr]eat room includes a fireplace, book-[cases] and a window wall. Adjacent to the

33

Design Z9822

First Floor: 1,944 square feet
Second Floor: 954 square feet
Total: 2,898 square feet

● This story-and-a-half home combines warm informal materials with a modern livable floor plan to create a true Southern classic. The dining room, study and great room work together to create one large, exciting space. Just beyond the open rail, the breakfast room is lined with windows. Plenty of counter space and storage make the kitchen truly usable. The master suite, with its tray ceiling and decorative wall niche, is a gracious and private owners' retreat. Upstairs, two additional bedrooms each have their own vanity within a shared bath while the third bedroom or guest room has its own bath and walk-in closet.

Design by
Design Traditions

WIDTH 51'-6"
DEPTH 73'

Design Z9867

First Floor: 1,554 square feet
Second Floor: 1,648 square feet
Total: 3,202 square feet

● The classic styling of this brick American traditional is defined by a double-door entrance with transom and Palladian window above. This opens to a grand foyer flanked by a spacious dining room and a formal study or parlor. A large family room with a full wall of glass opens conveniently to the kitchen and breakfast room. The master suite is on the second floor and features a sitting room with fireplace separated from the sleeping area by a majestic colonnade. Two additional bedrooms share a bath while a fourth has its own private bath.

Design by
Design Traditions

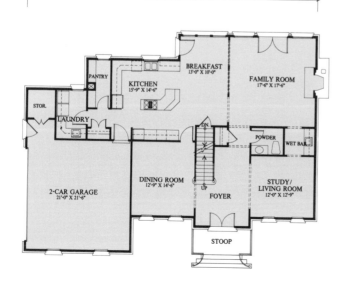

Design Z9837

First Floor: 1,847 square feet
Second Floor: 1,453 square feet
Total: 3,300 square feet

● To suit those who favor Classic European styling, this English Manor home features a dramatic brick exterior which is further emphasized by the varied roofline and the finial atop the uppermost gable. The main level opens with a two-story foyer and formal rooms on the right. The living room contains a fireplace set in a bay window. The dining room is separated from the living room by a symmetrical column arrangement. The more casual family room is to the rear. For guests, a bedroom and bath are located on the main level. The second floor provides additional bedrooms and baths for family as well as a magnificent master suite.

Design by
Design Traditions

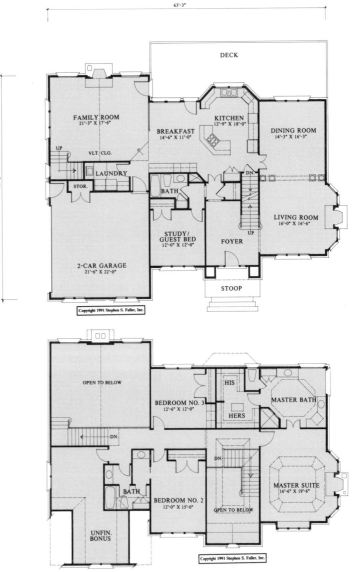

Design by
Design Traditions

Design Z9808
Square Footage: 2,902

● To highlight the exterior of this brick home, window jack arches have been artfully combined with arched transoms, gables and a sweeping roofline. The foyer opens into the formal dining room which is highlighted by the vaulted ceiling treatment and the stunning triple window. Also open to the foyer is the great room with its dramatic tray ceiling. The accommodating kitchen, with generous work island/breakfast bar, adjoins the breakfast area with its bright bay window and the keeping room with fireplace, vaulted ceiling and abundant windows. Two bedrooms and a connecting bath offering private vanities complete the rooms set along the front. The master suite with its garden bath and glass sitting room provides a quiet and peaceful retreat from the noise and pace of the day.

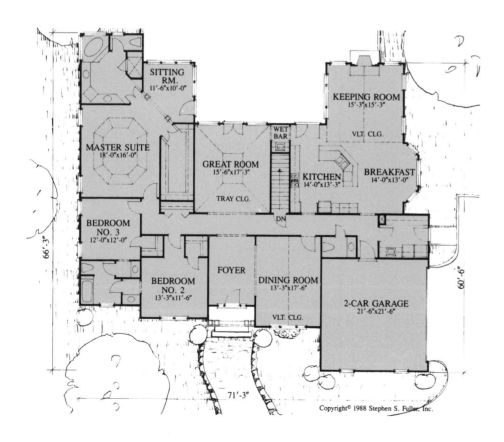

SITTING RM.
11'-6"x10'-0"

KEEPING ROOM
15'-3"x15'-3"

VLT. CLG.

MASTER SUITE
18'-0"x16'-0"

GREAT ROOM
15'-6"x17'-3"

WET BAR

KITCHEN
14'-0"x13'-3"

BREAKFAST
14'-0"x13'-0"

TRAY CLG.

66'-3"

DN

60'-6"

BEDROOM NO. 3
12'-0"x12'-0"

BEDROOM NO. 2
13'-3"x11'-6"

FOYER

DINING ROOM
13'-3"x17'-6"

2-CAR GARAGE
21'-6"x21'-6"

VLT. CLG.

71'-3"

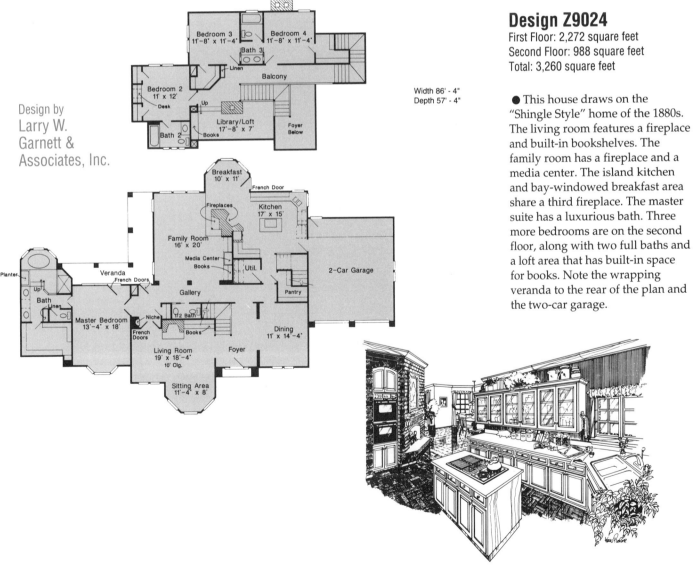

Bedroom 3
11'-8" x 11'-4"

Bedroom 4
11'-8" x 11'-4"

Bath 3

Linen

Bedroom 2
11' x 12'

Desk

Balcony

Up

Bath 2

Books

Library/Loft
17'-8" x 7'

Foyer Below

Design by
**Larry W.
Garnett &
Associates, Inc.**

Width 86' - 4"
Depth 57' - 4"

Breakfast
10' x 11'

French Door

Fireplaces

Kitchen
17' x 15'

Family Room
16' x 20'

Media Center
Books

Util.

2-Car Garage

Pantry

Planter

Veranda
French Doors

Gallery

Up

Bath
Linen

Master Bedroom
13'-4" x 18'

Niche
French Doors

1/2 Bath
Books

Living Room
19' x 18'-4"
10' Clg.

Foyer

Dining
11' x 14'-4"

Sitting Area
11'-4" x 8'

Design Z9024

First Floor: 2,272 square feet
Second Floor: 988 square feet
Total: 3,260 square feet

● This house draws on the "Shingle Style" home of the 1880s. The living room features a fireplace and built-in bookshelves. The family room has a fireplace and a media center. The island kitchen and bay-windowed breakfast area share a third fireplace. The master suite has a luxurious bath. Three more bedrooms are on the second floor, along with two full baths and a loft area that has built-in space for books. Note the wrapping veranda to the rear of the plan and the two-car garage.

Design Z8923

Square Footage: 2,361

● The combination of finely detailed brick and shingle siding recalls some of the distinctive architecture of the East Coast during the early part of this century. The foyer and gallery provide for a functional traffic pattern. The formal dining room to the front of the home is outlined by columns and features a 13-foot ceiling. The extensive living area offers a corner fireplace. A screened porch surrounding the breakfast room is an ideal entertainment area. The master suite features two spacious closets and a bath with a garden tub and an oversized shower. Bedroom 4 can serve as a study, nursery, guest room or home office.

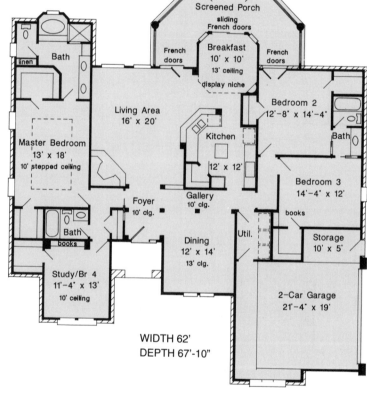

WIDTH 62'
DEPTH 67'-10"

9' ceiling throughout unless otherwise noted

Design by
Larry W.
Garnett &
Associates, Inc.

Design Z8922

First Floor: 2,242 square feet
Second Floor: 507 square feet
Total: 2,749 square feet

● Inspired by the turn-of-the-century homes along the Atlantic Coast, this design features finely detailed brickwork which is accented with shingle siding. The formal dining room is separated from traffic by three-foot walls. The grand two-story living room includes a sloped ceiling, a media center, a fireplace and circular stairs to the second floor. The gourmet kitchen overlooks the living area, breakfast room and a large covered porch. Three bedrooms include a master suite with spacious bath. The second floor offers a gameroom and a cozy study with dormer windows, a sloped ceiling and a built-in bookcase.

Design by
Larry W.
Garnett &
Associates, Inc.

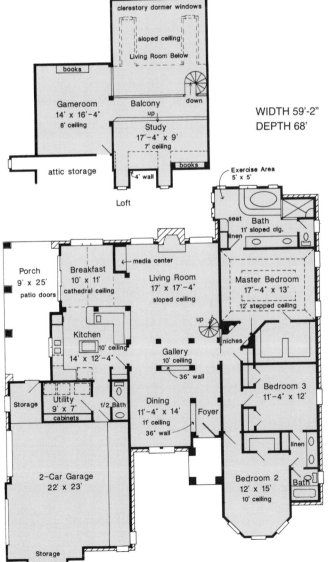

WIDTH 59'-2"
DEPTH 68'

REAR VIEW

Design Z9362
Square Footage: 2,172

● This one-story with grand rooflines holds a most convenient floor plan. The great room with fireplace to the rear complements a front-facing living room. The formal dining room with tray ceiling sits just across the hall from the living room and is also easily accessible to the kitchen. An island, pantry, breakfast room and patio are highlights in the kitchen. A bedroom with full bath at this end of the house works fine as an office or guest bedroom since a full bath is close by. Two additional bedrooms are to the right of the plan: a master suite with grand bath and one additional secondary bedroom. The three-car garage provides extra storage space.

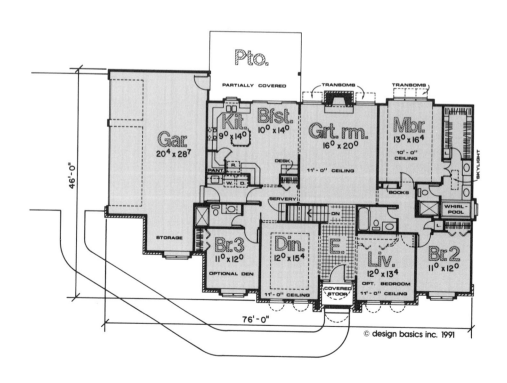

Design by
Design Basics, Inc.

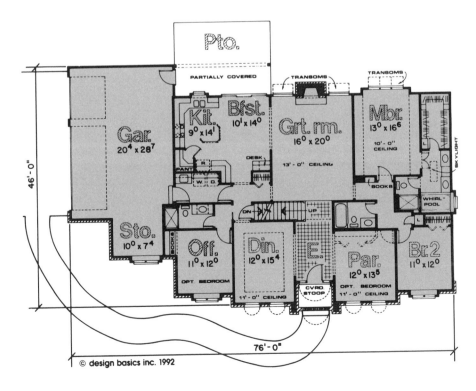

Br.3
10¹¹ x 15³/21⁷

Br.4
11⁰ x 10⁵/16⁹

DN

Pto.

PARTIALLY COVERED

TRANSOMS   TRANSOMS

Gar.
20⁴ x 28⁷

Kit.
9⁰ x 14¹

Bfst.
10¹ x 14⁰

Grt. rm.
16⁰ x 20⁰

13' - 0" CEILING

Mbr.
13⁰ x 16⁶

10' - 0"
CEILING

SKYLIGHT

DESK

PANT.

W D

BOOKS

WHIRL-
POOL

Sto.
10⁰ x 7⁴

BOOKS

DN   UP

Off.
11⁰ x 12⁰

OPT. BEDROOM

Din.
12⁰ x 15⁴

11' - 0" CEILING

E

CVRD.
STOOP

Par.
12⁰ x 13⁵

OPT. BEDROOM
11' - 0" CEILING

Br.2
11⁰ x 12⁰

46' - 0"

76' - 0"

Design Z9394

First Floor: 2,172 square feet
Second Floor: 595 square feet
Total: 2,767 square feet

● A covered stoop leads to an entry which offers a terrific view of the spacious great room featuring a volume ceiling and transom windows flanking the fireplace. Two first-floor rooms provide unmatched versatility as bedrooms or an office and parlor. A handsome kitchen with a Lazy Susan and an extra-wide island is complemented by a large walk-in pantry and an airy dinette. Three extra-high windows bring natural light into the spacious master bedroom. A large, walk-in closet adjoins a master bath featuring dual lavatories, separate whirlpool and shower areas and an attractive plant shelf. Two extra-deep second-floor bedrooms are joined by a full bath.

Design by

Design
Basics,
Inc.

Design Z3313

First Floor: 1,482 square feet
Second Floor: 885 square feet
Total: 2,367 square feet

● Cozy living abounds in a
first-floor living room and
family room, dining room,
and kitchen with breakfast
room. Two fireplaces keep
things warm. Three bed-
rooms upstairs have more
than adequate closet space.

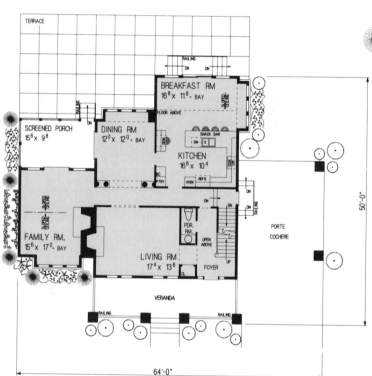

Design by
**Home Planners,
Inc.**

Federal, Georgian & Greek Revival Designs

Disciplined, highly symmetrical and geometrically precise are words to describe all three house styles—Federal, Georgian and Greek Revival. The Georgian Period began about 1700 and lasted until approximately 1870, when Late Georgian and Federal styles became more popular. The excavation of Pompeii led to interest in the Greek and Roman architecture and spawned the Greek Revival Period in America, which lasted from 1820 to 1860.

Georgian mansions are marked by symmetrical facades with precise alignment of windows, brick construction and massive chimneys. Paired end chimneys were common. The front door is a major feature in Georgian architecture, often flanked with plain or fluted pilasters or raised on pedestals with a simple triangular pediment overhead. From approximately 1760 to 1780, early Georgian architecture went through a period of transition from Late Georgian to Federal. Late Georgian made heavy use of classical details such as pilasters and columns.

The Federal Period lasted from 1780 to 1830. Particularly in the Northern colonies, builders kept the basic Roman symmetry present in Georgian design but eliminated much of the classical decoration. Federal doorways featured narrow flanking side lights and an elliptical fanlight. Federal designs remained elegant and grand, without the pretentiousness of Georgian design.

During the Greek Revival Period, designs resembled the Greek temple, with small, hidden windows, a white exterior, round Doric columns and entry porches. American architects frequently combined these details with other styles of architecture, creating Southern Colonial and other eclectic styles.

The designs in this section employ many classical details. They are grand, impressive homes with symmetrical facades, large chimneys and columns. The traditional exteriors are complemented by modern floor plans with all the amenities necessary for today's lifestyles.

Design Z9828

First Floor: 1,455 square feet
Second Floor: 1,649 square feet
Total: 3,104 square feet

● The double wings, twin chimneys and center portico of this home work in concert to create a classic architectural statement. The two-story foyer is flanked by the spacious dining room and formal living room, each containing its own fireplace. A large family room with a full wall of glass beckons the outside in while it opens conveniently onto the sunlit kitchen and breakfast room. The master suite features a tray ceiling and French doors that open onto a covered porch. A grand master bath with all the amenities, including garden tub and huge closet, completes the master suite. Two other bedrooms share a bath while another has its own private bath. The fourth bedroom also features a sunny nook for sitting or reading.

Design by
Design Traditions

WIDTH 53'
DEPTH 46'

WIDTH 77'-4"
DEPTH 58'-4"

Design Z9830

First Floor: 2,380 square feet
Second Floor: 1,295 square feet
Total: 3,675 square feet

● Blending of brick and finely crafted porches make this home a classic in traditional living. Past the large French doors, the impressive foyer is flanked by both the formal living and dining rooms. Beyond the stairhall is a vaulted great room with a wall of glass, a fireplace and accompanying bookcases. From here the breakfast room and kitchen are easily accessible and open onto their own private side porch. The master suite provides a large bath, two spacious closets, fireplace and a private entry that opens to the covered rear porch. The second floor has three bedrooms and a children's play room.

Design by
Design Traditions

Design Z9818 First Floor: 1,640 square feet; Second Floor: 1,030 square feet; Total: 2,670 square feet

● This home with its classic Georgian detailing features brick jack arches that frame the arched front door and windows. Dormers above and a motor-court entry garage add to the charm and elegance of this classically detailed home. Inside, the foyer leads directly to a large great room with a fireplace and French doors that lead outside. Just off the foyer, the dining room is separated by an open colonnade and receives brilliant light from the arched window. The kitchen and breakfast room with bay window offer every convenience including a handy cooking island and on-line work areas. Adjacent to the breakfast room is the keeping room which includes a corner fireplace and French doors that lead to the large rear porch. Comfort and privacy describe the master suite, complete with elegant tray ceilings, a large and accommodating bath and spacious walk-in closet. Upstairs, two additional bedrooms share convenient access to a bath while, down the hall, a fourth bedroom has its own private bath.

Design by
Design Traditions

WIDTH 53'
DEPTH 59'

Design by
Design Traditions

detail, the living and dining rooms are perfect for entertaining. The great room features a fireplace on the outside wall. This room opens to the breakfast room and angled kitchen with plenty of cabinets and counter space. Upstairs, is a guest room, a children's den area, two family bedrooms and master suite. Look for the cozy fireplace, tray ceiling and sumptuous bath in the master.

Design Z9814

First Floor: 1,370 square feet
Second Floor: 1,334 square feet
Total: 2,704 square feet

● This English Georgian home features a dramatic brick exterior. The series of windows and jack-arch detailing are second only to the drama created by the porte cochere. The detached garage allows the home to stretch to the gardens. Enter into the two-story foyer and the unusually shaped staircase and balcony overlook create a tremendous first impression. Separated only by a classical colonnade

Width 73'-6"
Depth 49'

● Fluted columns and decorative mouldings at the grand entrance present a stately, dignified exterior. A volume entry with graceful flared staircase opens to the formal dining room and parlor. The comfortable great room with boxed-beam ceiling and a raised-hearth fireplace is brightened by arched transom windows. A strategically located wet bar serves the dining room and the great room. The luxurious master suite includes a large walk-in closet and a spacious bath with whirlpool tub. A spacious media room with a built-in entertainment center is located on the second floor, along with three bedrooms and two full baths.

Design Z9382

First Floor: 1,923 square feet
Second Floor: 1,106 square feet
Total: 3,029 square feet

Design by
Design
Basics,
Inc.

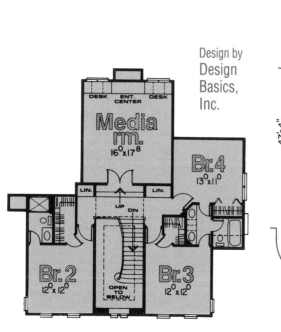

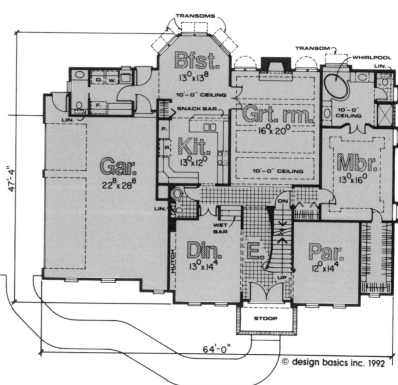

© design basics inc. 1992

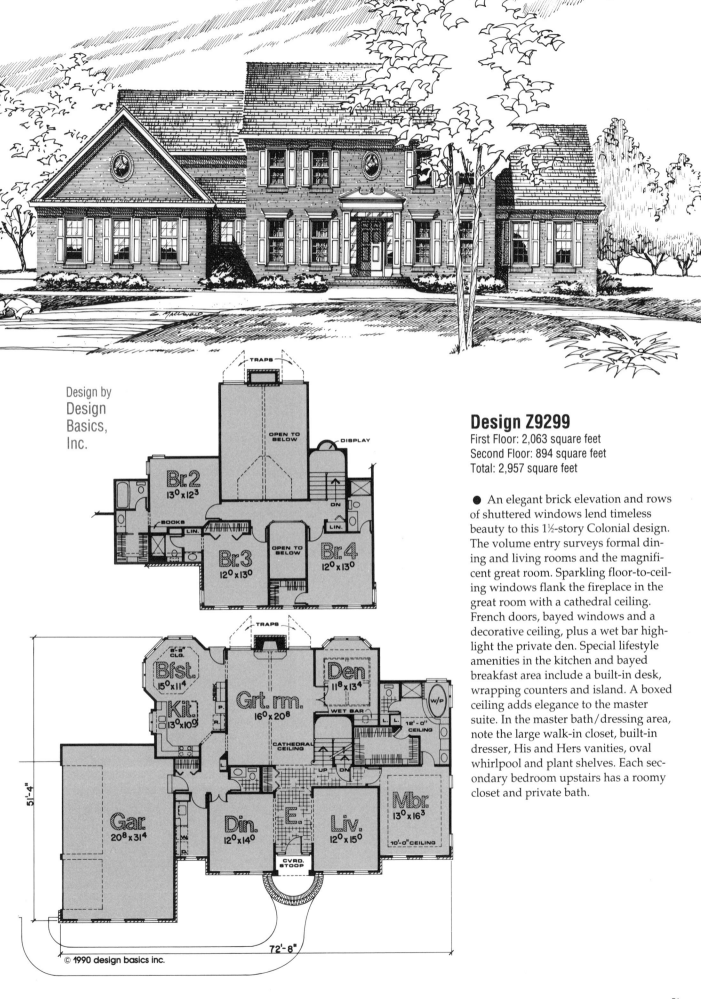

Design by
Design
Basics,
Inc.

TRAPS

OPEN TO BELOW

DISPLAY

Br.2
13⁰x12³

BOOKS
LIN.

Br.3
12⁰x13⁰

OPEN TO BELOW

Br.4
12⁰x13⁰

DN

LIN.

TRAPS

8'-6" CLG.

Bfst.
15⁰x11⁴

Kit.
13⁰x10⁹

Grt. rm.
16⁰x20⁸

Den
11⁸x13⁴

WET BAR

CATHEDRAL CEILING

W/P

12'-0" CEILING

UP   DN

Gar.
20⁸x31⁴

Din.
12⁰x14⁰

E.

Liv.
12⁰x15⁰

Mbr.
13⁰x16³

10'-0" CEILING

CVRD. STOOP

51'-4"

72'-8"

© 1990 design basics inc.

Design Z9299

First Floor: 2,063 square feet
Second Floor: 894 square feet
Total: 2,957 square feet

● An elegant brick elevation and rows of shuttered windows lend timeless beauty to this 1½-story Colonial design. The volume entry surveys formal dining and living rooms and the magnificent great room. Sparkling floor-to-ceiling windows flank the fireplace in the great room with a cathedral ceiling. French doors, bayed windows and a decorative ceiling, plus a wet bar highlight the private den. Special lifestyle amenities in the kitchen and bayed breakfast area include a built-in desk, wrapping counters and island. A boxed ceiling adds elegance to the master suite. In the master bath/dressing area, note the large walk-in closet, built-in dresser, His and Hers vanities, oval whirlpool and plant shelves. Each secondary bedroom upstairs has a roomy closet and private bath.

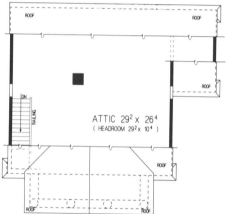

ATTIC 29² x 26⁴
(HEADROOM 29² x 10⁴)

BEDROOM 11⁰ x 10⁸

BATH DRESS RM

MASTER BEDROOM 13⁴ x 13⁴

BATH

LINEN

BEDROOM 10⁸ x 9²

BEDROOM 12⁰ x 10⁶

UPPER PORTICO

Design Z3339

First Floor: 1,460 square feet
Second Floor: 1,014 square feet
Total: 2,474 square feet

● This Colonial four-bedroom features the livable kind of plan you're looking for. A formal living room extends from the front foyer and leads to the formal dining area and nearby kitchen. A sunken family room has a raised-hearth fireplace. Three family bedrooms share a bath and are joined by the master bedroom with its own full bath.

Design by
Home Planners,
Inc.

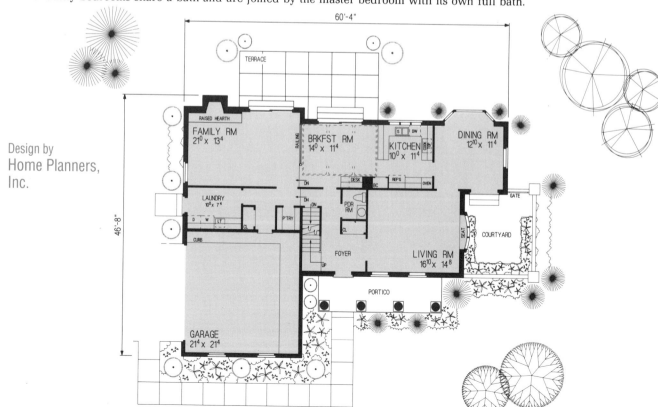

60'-4"

46'-8"

TERRACE

RAISED HEARTH

FAMILY RM 21⁰ x 13⁴

BRKFST RM 14⁰ x 11⁴

KITCHEN 10⁰ x 11⁴

DINING RM 12¹⁰ x 11⁴

LAUNDRY 10⁰ x 7⁴

DESK

REF'S

OVEN

P'TRY

POR RM

GATE

CURB

FOYER

SEAT

COURTYARD

LIVING RM 16¹⁰ x 14⁸

PORTICO

GARAGE 21⁰ x 21⁴

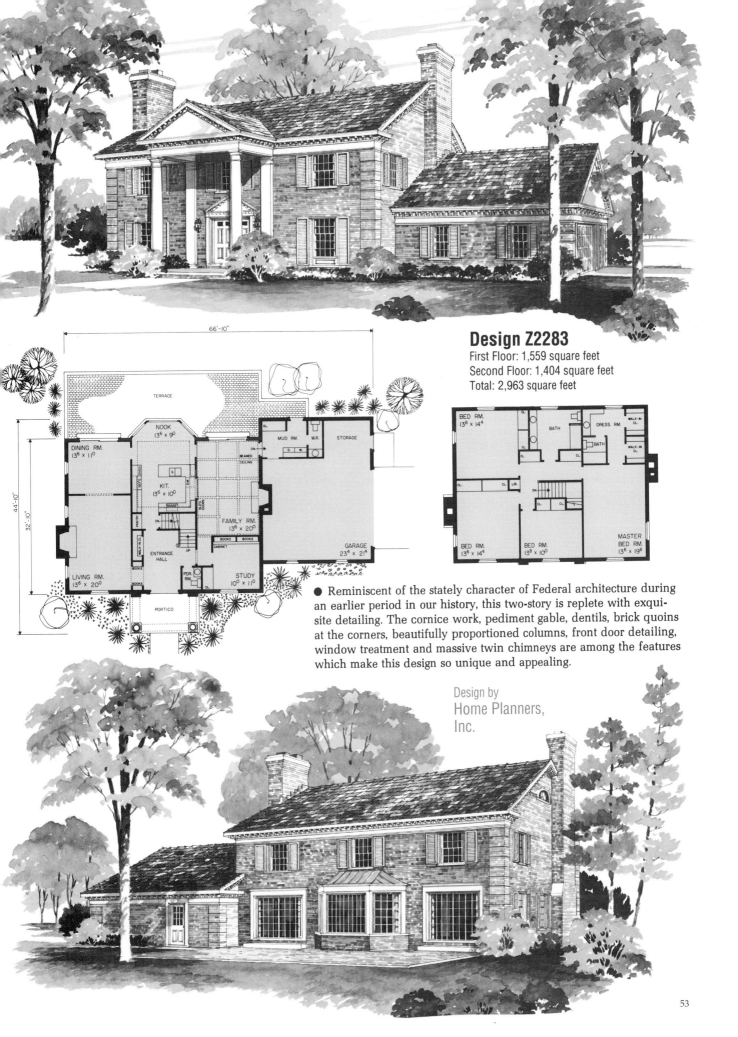

Design Z2283

First Floor: 1,559 square feet
Second Floor: 1,404 square feet
Total: 2,963 square feet

● Reminiscent of the stately character of Federal architecture during an earlier period in our history, this two-story is replete with exquisite detailing. The cornice work, pediment gable, dentils, brick quoins at the corners, beautifully proportioned columns, front door detailing, window treatment and massive twin chimneys are among the features which make this design so unique and appealing.

Design by
Home Planners,
Inc.

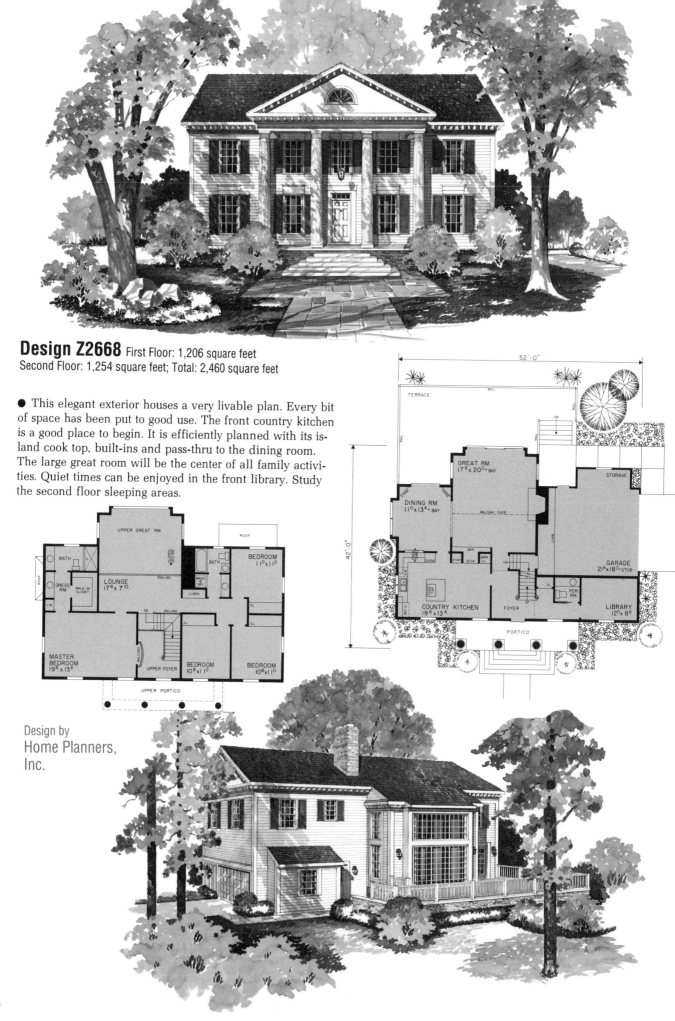

Design Z2668 First Floor: 1,206 square feet
Second Floor: 1,254 square feet; Total: 2,460 square feet

● This elegant exterior houses a very livable plan. Every bit of space has been put to good use. The front country kitchen is a good place to begin. It is efficiently planned with its island cook top, built-ins and pass-thru to the dining room. The large great room will be the center of all family activities. Quiet times can be enjoyed in the front library. Study the second floor sleeping areas.

Design by
Home Planners, Inc.

UPPER GREAT RM.

ROOF

BATH

DRESS. RM.

WALK-IN CLOSET

LOUNGE
17⁸ x 7¹⁰

BATH

WASH. & DRY

LINEN

BEDROOM
11⁰ x 11⁰

RAILING

DN
RAILING

BALCONY

CL

CL

CL

MASTER BEDROOM
19⁶ x 13⁴

UPPER FOYER

BEDROOM
10⁸ x 11⁰

BEDROOM
10⁸ x 11⁰

UPPER PORTICO

52'-0"

42'-0"

TERRACE

RAIL

DN

RAIL

GREAT RM.
17⁸ x 20⁰ + BAY

STORAGE

DINING RM.
11⁰ x 13⁴ + BAY

BALCONY OVER

BAR

OVENS

PTRY

DESK

BRM CL

DN

CL

CURB

GARAGE
21⁸ x 18⁰ + STOR.

REF.

COUNTRY KITCHEN
19⁶ x 13⁴

FOYER

UP

CL

PDR. RM.

LIBRARY
12⁰ x 8⁸

PORTICO

54

Design Z3333

First Floor: 1,584 square feet
Second Floor: 1,344 square feet
Total: 2,928 square feet

● This Southern Colonial adaptation boasts an up-to-date floor plan which caters to the needs of today's families. The entrance hall is flanked by formal and informal living areas: to the left a spacious living room and connecting dining room, to the right a cozy study and family room. A large kitchen with bay-windowed morning room is convenient to both the dining and family rooms. The upstairs sleeping area includes four bedrooms.

Design by
Home Planners,
Inc.

Design Z3353

First Floor: 2,191 square feet
Second Floor: 874 square feet
Total: 3,065 square feet

Design by
Home Planners,
Inc.

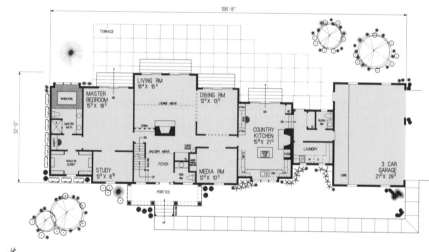

● This captivating 1½ story Southern Colonial provides the best in livability. On the first floor are the living room, dining room and private media room. A country kitchen with fireplace offers casual living space. The master suite is also located on this floor and has a lavish master bath with whirlpool spa. Upstairs are two family bedrooms, each with its own bath, and a central lounge overlooking the living room.

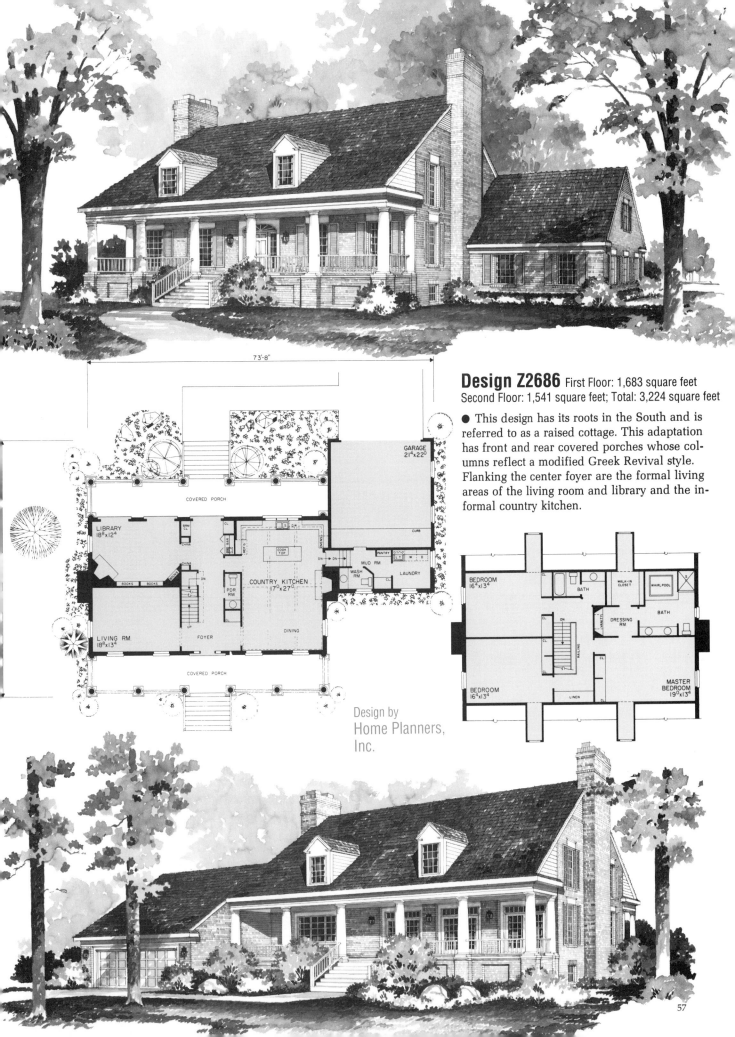

Design Z2686 First Floor: 1,683 square feet
Second Floor: 1,541 square feet; Total: 3,224 square feet

● This design has its roots in the South and is referred to as a raised cottage. This adaptation has front and rear covered porches whose columns reflect a modified Greek Revival style. Flanking the center foyer are the formal living areas of the living room and library and the informal country kitchen.

Design by
Home Planners,
Inc.

73'-8"

GARAGE
21⁴x22⁰

COVERED PORCH

LIBRARY
18⁸x12⁴

CURB

CHINA

PANTRY

COOK TOP

MUD RM

COUNTRY KITCHEN
17⁰x27⁰

WASH RM

LAUNDRY

BOOKS   BOOKS

PDR RM

LIVING RM.
18⁸x13⁴

FOYER

UP

DINING

COVERED PORCH

BEDROOM
16⁴x13⁴

BATH

WALK-IN CLOSET

WHIRLPOOL

BATH

DN

DRESSING RM

BEDROOM
16⁴x13⁴

LINEN

RAILING

MASTER BEDROOM
19⁰x13⁴

Design by
Design Traditions

Great Room Interior Elevation

Design Z9806
Square Footage: 2,697

● Dual chimneys (one a false chimney created to enhance the aesthetic effect) and a double stairway to the covered entry of this home create a balanced architectural statement. The sunlit foyer leads straight into the spacious great room, where French doors and large side windows provide a generous view of the covered veranda in back. The great room features a tray ceiling and a fireplace, bordered by twin bookcases. Another great view is offered from the spacious kitchen with breakfast bar and a roomy work island. The master suite provides a large balanced bath, a spacious closet, and a glassed sitting area with access to the veranda.

WIDTH 65'-3"
DEPTH 67'-3"

Design Z9804

First Floor: 2,199 square feet
Second Floor: 1,235 square feet
Total: 3,434 square feet

● The covered front porch of this home warmly welcomes family and visitors. To the right of the foyer is a versatile option room. On the other side is the formal dining room, located just across from the open great room with its skylights, French doors and fireplace—which also opens into the breakfast room. The kitchen with its bay window includes a cooking island/ breakfast bar. Adjacent to the breakfast room is the sun room. At the rear of the main level is the master suite, which features a decorative tray ceiling and a lavish bath loaded with features. Just off the bedroom is a private deck. On the second level, three additional bedrooms and two baths are found.

WIDTH 62'-6"
DEPTH 54'-3"

Design by
Design Traditions

Design Z9087

First Floor: 2,263 square feet
Second Floor: 787 square feet
Total: 3,050 square feet

Design by
Larry W.
Garnett &
Associates, Inc.

● Excellent outdoor living is yours with this 1½-story home. The wrapping covered front porch gives way to a center hall entry with flanking living and dining rooms. The living room features a media center, two-way fireplace and columned entry. The attached garden room has French doors to the front porch and French doors to a smaller covered porch that is also accessed through the master bedroom suite. The family room is complemented by a fireplace, built-in bookshelves and another covered porch. An angled island counter separates it from the kitchen. Upstairs are three bedrooms and two full baths. Bedroom 4 has a beautiful bumped out window while Bedrooms 2 and 3 have dormer windows.

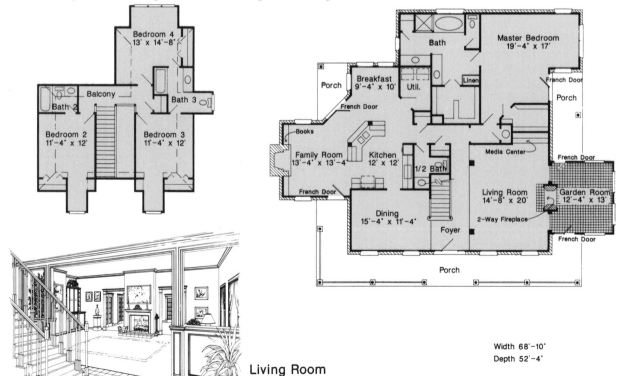

Living Room

Width 68'-10"
Depth 52'-4"

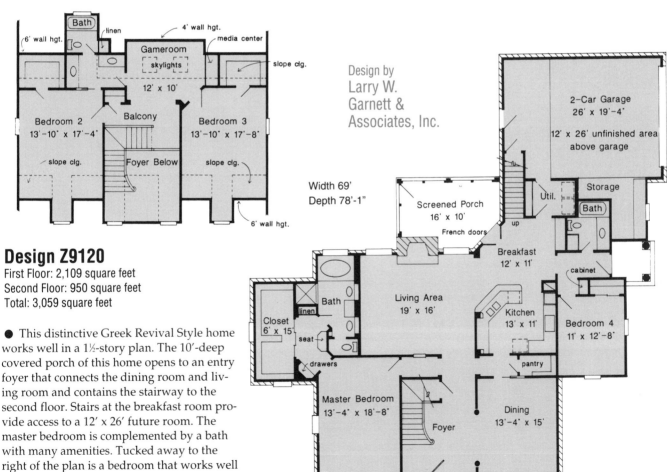

Bath

linen

6' wall hgt.

4' wall hgt.

media center

Gameroom

skylights

12' x 10'

slope clg.

Bedroom 2
13'-10" x 17'-4"

Balcony

Bedroom 3
13'-10" x 17'-8"

slope clg.

Foyer Below

slope clg.

6' wall hgt.

Design by
Larry W.
Garnett &
Associates, Inc.

2-Car Garage
26' x 19'-4"

12' x 26' unfinished area
above garage

Width 69'
Depth 78'-1"

Screened Porch
16' x 10'

French doors

Util.

up

Storage

Bath

Breakfast
12' x 11'

cabinet

Living Area
19' x 16'

Kitchen
13' x 11'

Bath

Closet
6' x 15'

linen

Bedroom 4
11' x 12'-8"

seat

drawers

pantry

Master Bedroom
13'-4" x 18'-8"

Foyer

Dining
13'-4" x 15'

Porch
40' x 10'

Design Z9120

First Floor: 2,109 square feet
Second Floor: 950 square feet
Total: 3,059 square feet

● This distinctive Greek Revival Style home works well in a 1½-story plan. The 10'-deep covered porch of this home opens to an entry foyer that connects the dining room and living room and contains the stairway to the second floor. Stairs at the breakfast room provide access to a 12' x 26' future room. The master bedroom is complemented by a bath with many amenities. Tucked away to the right of the plan is a bedroom that works well as guest quarters or could hold a home office or study. For additional sleeping space, there are two bedrooms with dormer windows and walk-in closets, plus a full bath on the second floor.

Design Z9375

Square Footage: 2,456

● Tapered columns at the entry help to create a majestic front elevation. Inside, an open great room features a wet bar, a fireplace, tall windows and access to a covered porch with skylights. A wide kitchen features an ideally placed island, two pantries and easy laundry access. Double doors open to the master suite where attention is drawn to French doors leading to the master bath and the covered porch. The master bath provides beauty and convenience with a whirlpool, dual lavatories, plant shelves and a large walk-in closet. Two secondary bedrooms share a compartmented bath.

Design by
Design
Basics,
Inc.

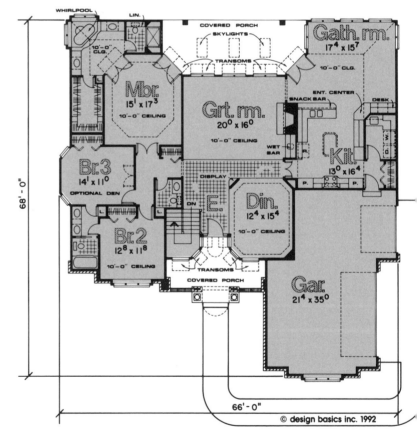

Br. 4
12⁰ x 13³

SEAT

LIN

OPT. BEDROOM

Design Z9396

Square Footage: 2,775

● An impressive wrought iron-accented entry introduces a captivating courtyard. The dignified surroundings of the formal dining room enhance entertaining. Family living is highlighted in the integrated design of the kitchen, breakfast bay and family room. The huge laundry room is well-planned and placed for efficiency and convenience. For maximum privacy, double doors seclude the bedroom wing from the rest of the house. The master suite includes a built-in dresser, outdoor access and a private sitting room. The master bath with dual lavatories and extra-large oval whirlpool is distinguished by a multi-faceted sloped ceiling.

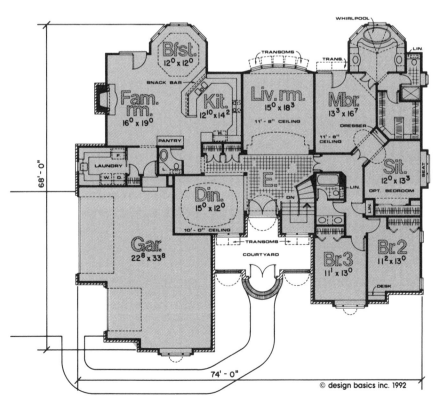

Bfst.
12⁰ x 12⁰

SNACK BAR

WHIRLPOOL

Fam.
rm.
16⁰ x 19⁰

Kit.
12¹⁰ x 14²

Liv. rm.
15⁰ x 18³

11' - 8" CEILING

Mbr.
13³ x 16⁷

DRESSER

11' - 8" CEILING

LIN

TRANS.

TRANSOMS

PANTRY

LAUNDRY

W D

Din.
15⁰ x 12⁰

10' - 0" CEILING

E.

DN

Sit.
12⁰ x 13³

OPT. BEDROOM

SEAT

LIN

LIN

Gar.
22⁸ x 33⁸

COURTYARD

TRANSOMS

Br. 3
11' x 13⁰

Br. 2
11² x 13⁰

DESK

68' - 0"

74' - 0"

© design basics inc. 1992

Design by
Design
Basics,
Inc.

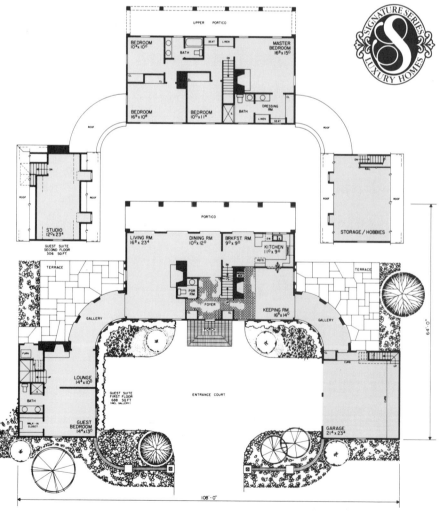

Design Z2665

First Floor: 1,152 square feet
Second Floor: 1,152 square feet
Total: 2,304 square feet
(Excludes Guest Suite and Galleries)

● This magnificent manor's street view illustrates a centralized mansion connected by curving galleries to matching wings. The origin of this house dates back to 1787 and George Washington's Mount Vernon. The underlying aesthetics for this design come from the rational balancing of porticos, fenestration and chimneys. Six two-story columns, along with four sets of French doors, highlight the rear elevation. The living room encompasses the entire width of the house. Four bedrooms, including a master suite with a fireplace, are on the second floor.

Design by
Home Planners, Inc.

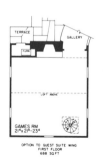

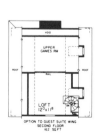

Victorian Home Plans

After the formality and symmetry of the Greek Revival period, designers began to experiment and incorporate curved lines and exotic details in public and private buildings. So arose the Victorian style, characterized by freedom of expression, liveliness, whimsy and optimism. Named after Queen Victoria, who reigned from 1837 to 1901, the Victorian Period spanned seven decades from 1840 to 1910.

Victorian architecture includes an array of styles, characterized by asymmetrical two-story facades, large chimneys, multiple projections, contrasting wall materials, porches and elaborate ornamentation.

Gothic Revival (1840 to 1880) and Italianate style (1840 to 1885) marked the beginning of the Victorian Period. A steeply pitched roof with cross gables and decorative trim pieces called vergeboards exemplified Gothic Revival. Italianate style emphasized Italian villa-style architecture with low-pitched roofs, a central tower, wide overhangs and tall, narrow windows, often covered with hooded crowns or eyebrows.

The Middle Victorian Period brought the Second Empire and Stick styles. Second Empire, or Mansardic, homes offered the dual-pitched, hipped mansard roof named after 17th-Century French architect Francois Mansart. Wood replaced masonry in the building of Stick houses. Walls were decorated with varying patterns of horizontal, vertical or diagonal boards raised from the wall surface.

The High Victorian Period culminated in the Queen Anne Style, typified by elaborate detailing including patterned shingles, carved fretwork, finials, and spindlework. Many Queen Anne Victorians are found in the San Francisco area. Splendid Queen Anne Victorians and Victorian designs of all types are included in this section.

Design Z2970 First Floor: 1,538 square feet
Second Floor: 1,526 square feet; Third Floor: 658 square feet
Total: 3,722 square feet

● A porch, is a porch, is a porch. But, when it wraps around to a side, or even two sides, of the house, we have called it a veranda. This charming Victorian features a covered outdoor living area on all four sides! It even ends at a screened porch which features a sun deck above. This interesting plan offers three floors of livability. And what livability it is! Plenty of formal and informal living facilities to go along with the potential of five bedrooms. The master suite is just that. It is adjacent to an interesting sitting room. It has a sun deck and excellent bath/personal care facilities. The third floor will make a wonderful haven for the family's student members.

Design by
Home Planners, Inc.

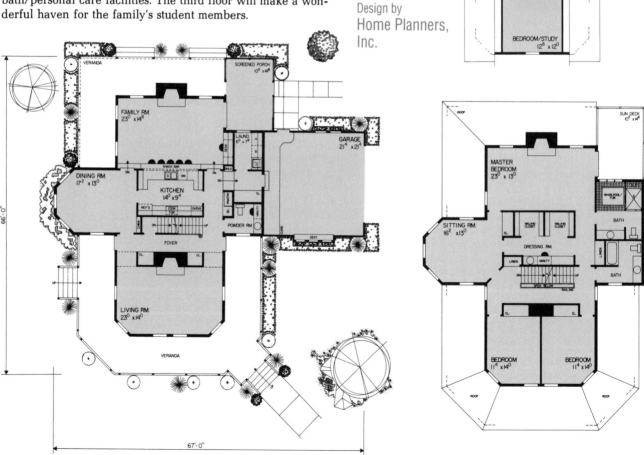

Design Z3309

First Floor: 1,375 square feet
Second Floor: 1,016 square feet
Total: 2,391 square feet

● Covered porches, front and back, are a fine preview to the livable nature of this Victorian. Living areas are defined in a family room with fireplace, formal living and dining rooms, and a kitchen with breakfast room. An ample laundry room, garage with storage area, and powder room round out the first floor. Three second floor bedrooms are joined by a study and two full baths.

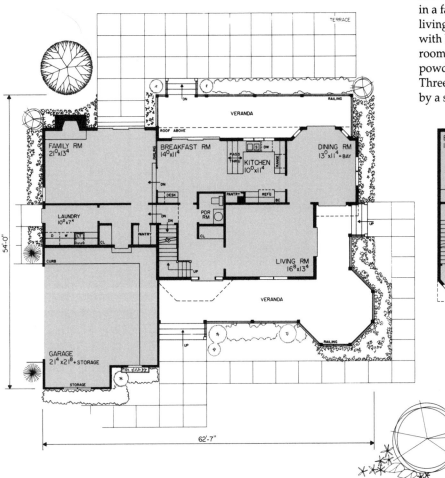

Design by
Home Planners,
Inc.

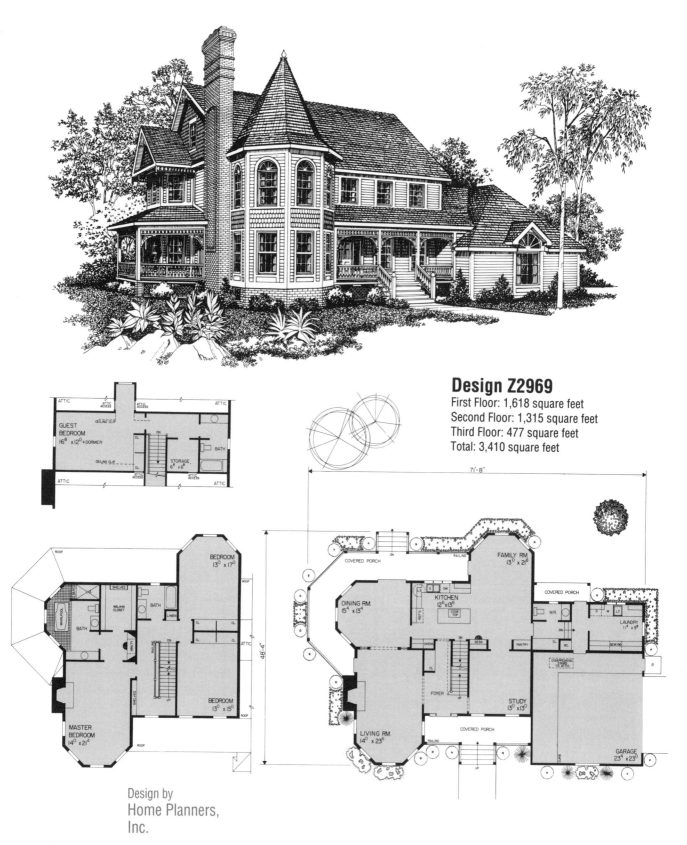

Design Z2969

First Floor: 1,618 square feet
Second Floor: 1,315 square feet
Third Floor: 477 square feet
Total: 3,410 square feet

Design by
Home Planners,
Inc.

● What could beat the charm of a turreted Victorian with covered porches to the front, side and rear? This delicately detailed exterior houses an outstanding family oriented floor plan. Projecting bays make their contribution to the exterior styling. In addition, they provide an extra measure of livability

to the living, dining and family rooms, plus two of the bedrooms. The efficient kitchen, with its island cooking station, functions well with the dining and family rooms. A study provides a quiet first floor haven for the family's less active pursuits. Upstairs there are three big bedrooms and a fine master bath.

The third floor provides a guest suite and huge bulk storage area (make it a cedar closet if you wish). This house has a basement for the development of further recreational and storage facilities. Don't miss the two fireplaces, large laundry and attached two-car garage. A great investment.

Design Z2973

First Floor: 1,269 square feet
Second Floor: 1,227 square feet
Total: 2,496 square feet

● A most popular feature of the Victorian house has always been its covered porches. In addition to being an appealing exterior design feature, covered porches have their practical side, too. They provide wonderful indoor-outdoor living relationships. Imagine, sheltered outdoor living facilities for the various formal and informal living and dining areas of the plan. The family will enjoy the bayed family room as well as the arrangement of upstairs bedrooms. The master suite features a bath with a whirlpool while the other bedrooms share a bath with dual vanities. For information on customizing this design, call 1-800-322-6769, ext. 800.

Design by
Home Planners,
Inc.

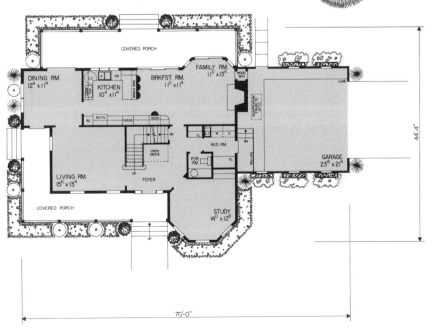

Design Z3389 First Floor: 1,161 square feet; Second Floor: 1,090 square feet; Third Floor: 488 square feet; Total: 2,739 square feet

● A stunning Victorian turret accents the facade of this compact three-story beauty, a promise of the exciting floor plan held inside. Downstairs rooms include a grand-sized living room/dining room combination that handles both formal and infor-mal gatherings. The U-shaped kitchen has a snack-bar pass-through to the dining room. Just to the left of the entry foyer is a private study with wet bar. On the second floor are three bedrooms and two full baths. The master bedroom has a whirlpool spa and large walk-in closet. The third floor is a perfect location for a guest bedroom with private bath, dormer window and two closets. Be sure to note the full-width covered porch stretching across the back of the house.

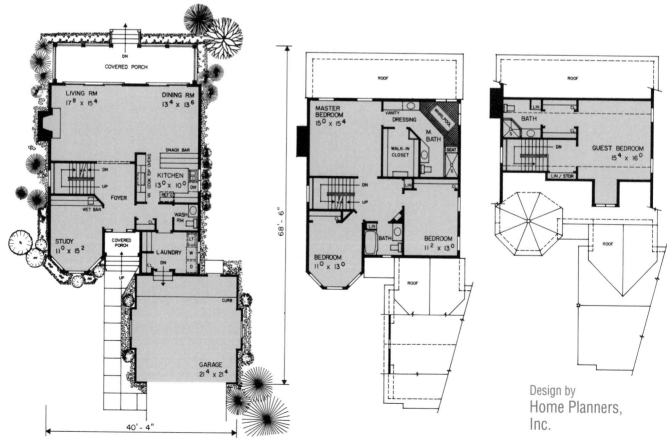

Design by
Home Planners,
Inc.

Design Z3393

First Floor: 1,449 square feet
Second Floor: 902 square feet
Total: 2,351 square feet

● A turreted facade, dormer window and fish-scale shingle details make this moderately sized Victorian stand out at a glance. Its well-designed floor plan makes it even more attractive. Notice how guests as well as family are accommodated: powder room in the front foyer; gathering room with terrace access, fireplace and attached formal dining room; split-bedroom sleeping arrangements. The master suite contains His and Hers walk-in closets, a separate shower and whirlpool tub and a delightful bay-windowed area. Upstairs there are three more bedrooms (one could serve as a study, one as a media room), a full bath and an open lounge area overlooking the gathering room. Notice the covered porches front and rear and long terrace area.

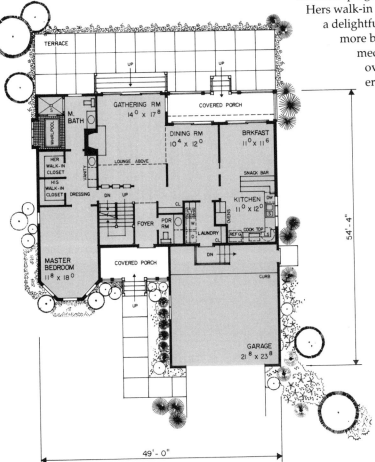

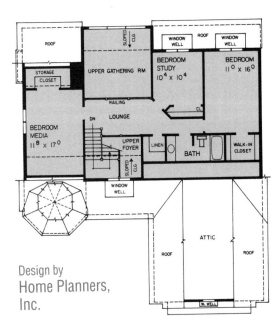

Design by
Home Planners,
Inc.

Design Z9012

First Floor: 1,357 square feet
Second Floor: 1,079 square feet
Total: 2,436 square feet

● An inviting wraparound veranda with delicate spindlework and a raised turret with leaded-glass windows recall the grand Queen Anne Victorians of the late 1880s. Double doors open from the dramatic two-story foyer to a private study with built-in bookcases and a bay window. The gallery, with decorative wood columns and an arched ceiling, overlooks both the large formal dining and living rooms. French doors open from the living room to the front veranda and to the screened porch. A fireplace adds warmth to the breakfast area and the island kitchen. Above the two-car garage is an optional area that is perfect for a home office or guest quarters. Upstairs, the master suite, with His and Hers walk-in closets, leads to a luxurious bath with a garden tub and glass-enclosed shower. An optional exercise loft and plant shelves complete this elegant master bath. Two additional bedrooms, one with a private deck and the other with a cathedral ceiling, share a dressing area and bath.

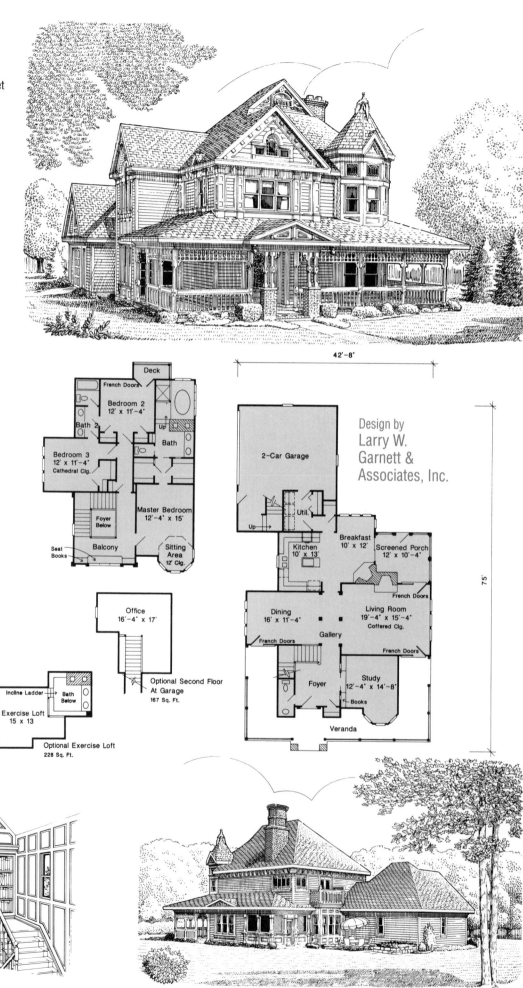

Design by
Larry W. Garnett & Associates, Inc.

42'-8"

75'

Second Floor:
Deck
French Doors
Bedroom 2 12' x 11'-4"
Bath 2
Up
Bath
Bedroom 3 12' x 11'-4" Cathedral Clg.
Foyer Below
Seat Books
Balcony
Master Bedroom 12'-4" x 15'
Sitting Area 12' Clg.

First Floor:
2-Car Garage
Up
Util.
Kitchen 10' x 13'
Breakfast 10' x 12'
Screened Porch 12' x 10'-4"
French Doors
Dining 16' x 11'-4"
Gallery
Living Room 19'-4" x 15'-4" Coffered Clg.
French Doors
French Doors
Foyer
Study 12'-4" x 14'-8"
Books
Veranda

Optional Office:
Office 16'-4" x 17'
Optional Second Floor At Garage 167 Sq. Ft.

Incline Ladder
Bath Below
Exercise Loft 15 x 13
Optional Exercise Loft 228 Sq. Ft.

Design Z9014

First Floor: 1,565 square feet
Second Floor: 1,598 square feet
Total: 3,163 square feet

● The angled entry of this home opens to a grand foyer and a formal parlor with expansive windows and a French door leading to the side yard. The formal dining area features a built-in hutch. Double French doors open from the foyer to the large study with bookcases and full-length windows. The spacious family room with a fireplace and wet bar is a superb entertainment area. The kitchen with its work island and abundant cabinet space overlooks the octagon-shaped breakfast room. Upstairs, the master bedroom has French doors which open onto a rear deck. The distinctive bath features a bay-windowed tub area and glass enclosed shower. Three additional bedrooms each have walk-in closets. Plans for two-car detached garage are included.

Design by
Larry W.
Garnett &
Associates, Inc.

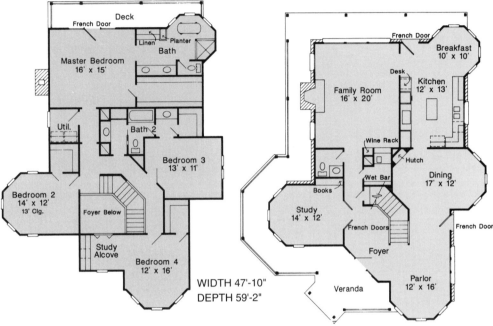

Deck
French Door
Linen
Planter
Bath
Master Bedroom
16' x 15'
Util.
Bath 2
Bedroom 3
13' x 11'
Bedroom 2
14' x 12'
13' Clg.
Foyer Below
Study Alcove
Bedroom 4
12' x 16'

WIDTH 47'-10"
DEPTH 59'-2"

French Door
Breakfast
10' x 10'
Desk
Family Room
16' x 20'
Kitchen
12' x 13'
Wine Rack
Hutch
Wet Bar
Dining
17' x 12'
Books
Study
14' x 12'
French Doors
Foyer
French Door
Veranda
Parlor
12' x 16'

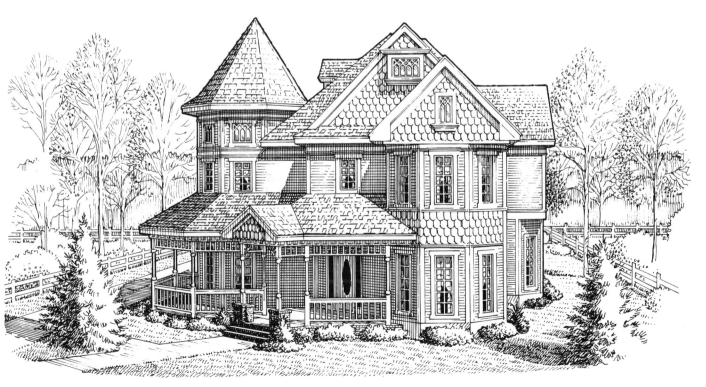

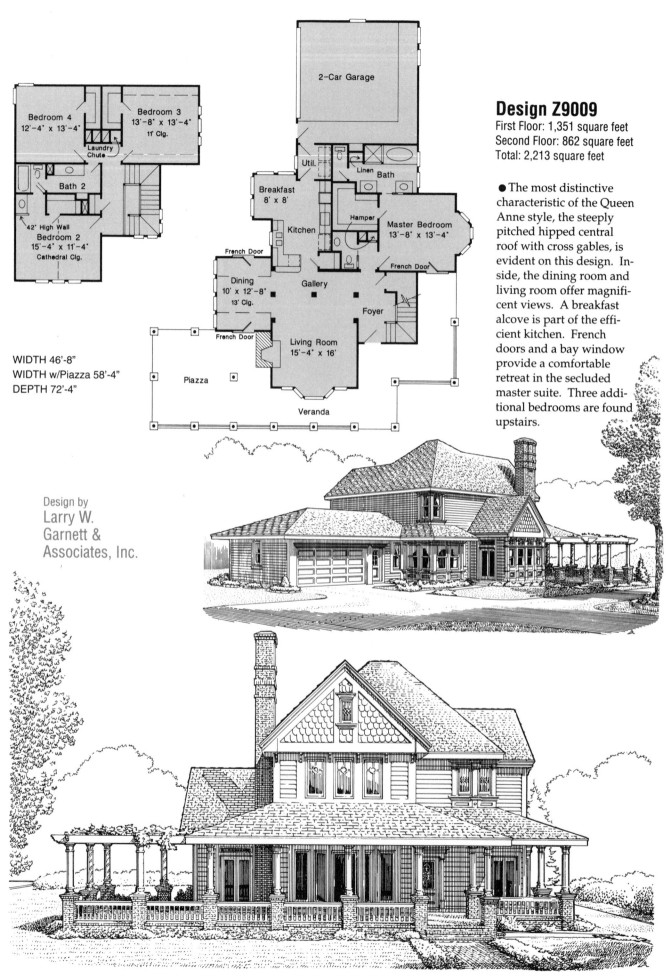

Bedroom 4
12'-4" x 13'-4"

Bedroom 3
13'-8" x 13'-4"
11' Clg.

Laundry Chute

Bath 2

42" High Wall

Bedroom 2
15'-4" x 11'-4"
Cathedral Clg.

WIDTH 46'-8"
WIDTH w/Piazza 58'-4"
DEPTH 72'-4"

Design by
Larry W.
Garnett &
Associates, Inc.

2-Car Garage

Util.

Linen   Bath

Breakfast
8' x 8'

Hamper

Master Bedroom
13'-8" x 13'-4"

Kitchen

French Door

French Door

Dining
10' x 12'-8"
13' Clg.

Gallery

Foyer

French Door

Living Room
15'-4" x 16'

Piazza

Veranda

Design Z9009

First Floor: 1,351 square feet
Second Floor: 862 square feet
Total: 2,213 square feet

● The most distinctive characteristic of the Queen Anne style, the steeply pitched hipped central roof with cross gables, is evident on this design. Inside, the dining room and living room offer magnificent views. A breakfast alcove is part of the efficient kitchen. French doors and a bay window provide a comfortable retreat in the secluded master suite. Three additional bedrooms are found upstairs.

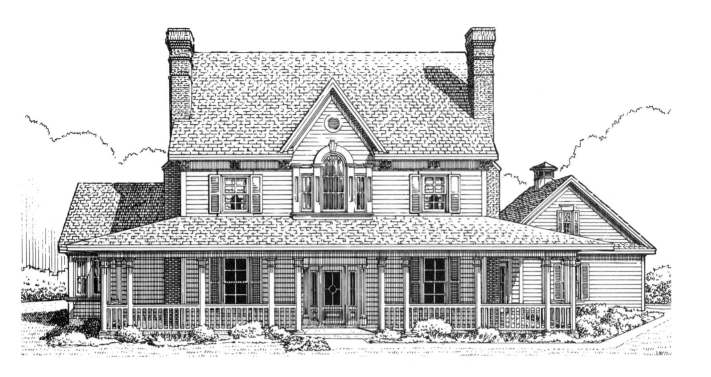

Design Z9067

First Floor: 1,999 square feet
Second Floor: 933 square feet
Total: 2,932 square feet

● The wraparound veranda and simple lines give this home an unassuming elegance that is characteristic of its Folk Victorian heritage. Opening directly to the formal dining room, the two-story foyer offers extra space for large dinner parties. Double French doors lead to the study with raised paneling and a cozy fireplace. Built-in bookcases conceal a hidden security vault. The private master suite features a corner garden tub, glass-enclosed shower and a walk-in closet. Overlooking the family room and built-in breakfast nook is the central kitchen. A rear staircase provides convenient access to the second floor from the family room. The balcony provides a view of the foyer below and the Palladian window. Three additional bedrooms complete this exquisite home.

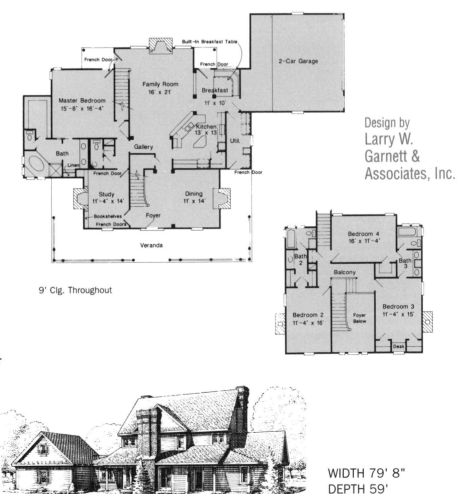

Design by
Larry W.
Garnett &
Associates, Inc.

WIDTH 79' 8"
DEPTH 59'

REAR VIEW

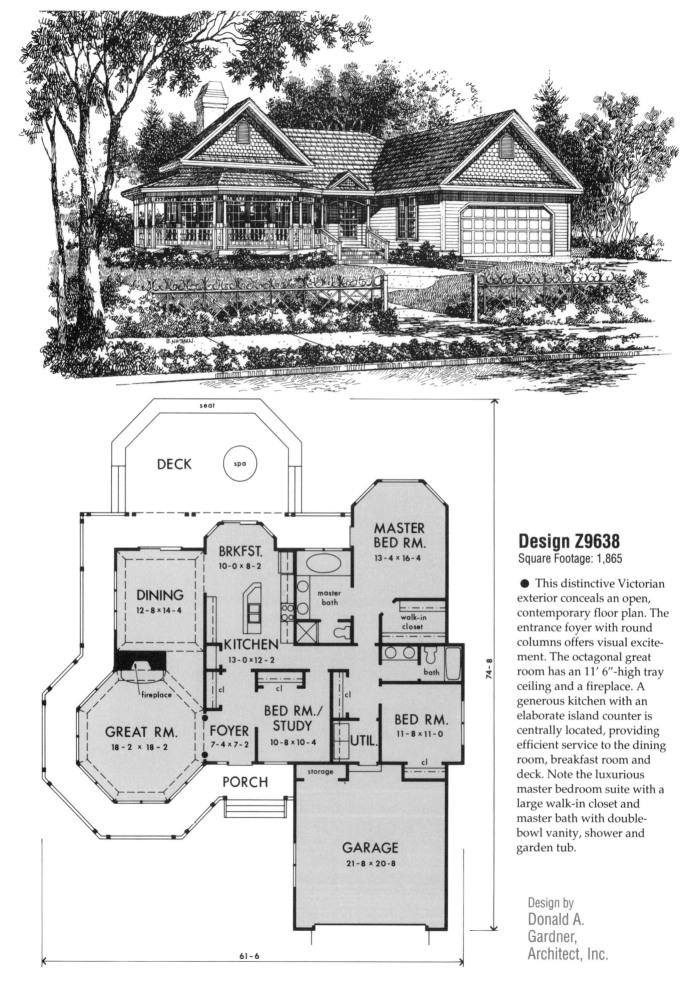

DECK

seat

spa

BRKFST.
10-0 x 8-2

DINING
12-8 x 14-4

master
bath

MASTER
BED RM.
13-4 x 16-4

walk-in
closet

KITCHEN
13-0 x 12-2

bath

fireplace

cl

cl

cl

GREAT RM.
18-2 x 18-2

FOYER
7-4 x 7-2

BED RM./
STUDY
10-8 x 10-4

UTIL.

BED RM.
11-8 x 11-0

cl

PORCH

storage

74-8

GARAGE
21-8 x 20-8

61-6

Design Z9638
Square Footage: 1,865

● This distinctive Victorian exterior conceals an open, contemporary floor plan. The entrance foyer with round columns offers visual excitement. The octagonal great room has an 11′ 6″-high tray ceiling and a fireplace. A generous kitchen with an elaborate island counter is centrally located, providing efficient service to the dining room, breakfast room and deck. Note the luxurious master bedroom suite with a large walk-in closet and master bath with double-bowl vanity, shower and garden tub.

Design by
Donald A.
Gardner,
Architect, Inc.

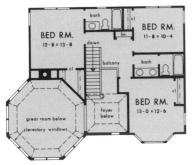

Design by
Donald A.
Gardner,
Architect, Inc.

Design Z9699

First Floor: 1,519 square feet
Second Floor: 792 square feet
Total: 2,311 square feet

Design Z9698

First Floor: 1,790 square feet
Second Floor: 792 square feet
Total: 2,582 square feet

● One great exterior; two floor plans. The second floor is the same for both plans—the difference lies only in the first-floor layout. It features a great room and formal dining room on Design Z9699; a formal living room, dining room and family room on Design Z9698. Order Design Z9698 for living room option; order Design Z9699 for great room option.

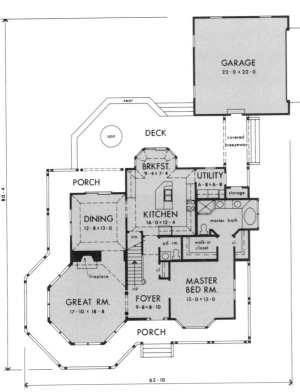

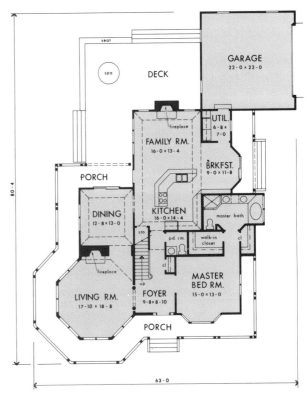

Design Z9232

First Floor: 1,551 square feet
Second Floor: 725 square feet
Total: 2,276 square feet

● This narrow-lot plan features a wraparound porch at the two-story entry, which opens to the formal dining room with beautiful bay windows. The great room features a handsome fireplace and a ten-and-a-half foot ceiling. A well-equipped island kitchen with pantry and built-in desk is available for the serious cook. The large master bedroom has a vaulted ceiling and a luxury master bath with two-person whirlpool, skylight and large walk-in closet. Three secondary bedrooms with ample closet space share a compartmented bath including double vanity and a large linen closet.

Design by
Design
Basics,
Inc.

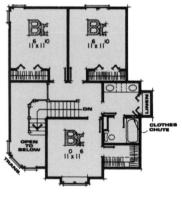

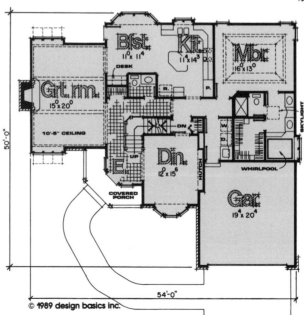

© 1989 design basics inc.

78

Design Z9251

First Floor: 1,653 square feet
Second Floor: 700 square feet
Total: 2,353 square feet

● Beautiful arches and elaborate detail give the elevation of this four-bedroom, 1½-story home an unmistakable elegance. Inside the floor plan is equally appealing. Note the formal dining room with bay window, visible from the entrance hall. The large great room has a fireplace and a wall of windows out the back. A hearth room, with bookcase, adjoins the kitchen area with walk-in pantry. The master suite on the first floor features His and Hers wardrobes, a large whirlpool and double lavatories. Upstairs quarters share a full bath with compartmented sinks.

Design by
Design
Basics,
Inc.

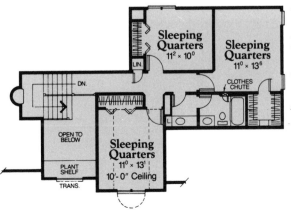

© 1990 design basics inc.

Design Z3384 First Floor: 1,399 square feet
Second Floor: 1,123 square feet; Total: 2,522 square feet

● Classic Victorian styling comes to the forefront in this Queen Anne two-story. Complementary fishscale-adorned pediments top the bayed tower to the left and garage to the right. Smaller versions are found at the dormer windows above a spindlework porch. The interior boasts comfortable living quarters for the entire family. On opposite sides of the wide foyer are the formal dining and living rooms. To the rear, is a country-style island kitchen with attached family room (don't miss the fireplace here). A small library shares a covered porch with this informal gathering area and also has its own fireplace. Thr[ee] bedrooms on the second floor include a master suite with grand bath. The two f[am]ily bedrooms share a full bath. Take spe[cial] note of the service area conveniently attached to the two-car garage.

Design by
Home Planners,
Inc.

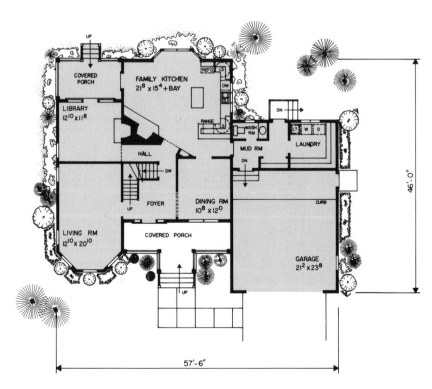

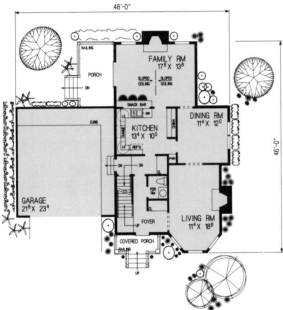

Design Z3383

First Floor: 995 square feet
Second Floor: 1,064 square feet
Third Floor: 425 square feet
Total: 2,484 square feet

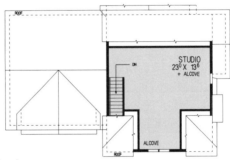

Design by
Home Planners,
Inc.

● This delightful Victorian cottage features three floors of living potential and exterior details that perfectly complement the convenient plan inside. Note the central placement of the kitchen, near to the dining room and the family room. A lovely side porch is the ideal location for weekend relaxing. Two fireplaces keep things warm and cozy. Three second-floor bedrooms include a master suite with bay window and two family bedrooms, one with an alcove and walk-in closet. Use the third-floor studio as a study, office or playroom for the children.

Design Z3382

First Floor: 1,366 square feet
Second Floor: 837 square feet
Third Floor: 363 square feet
Total: 2,566 square feet

Design by
Home Planners,
Inc.

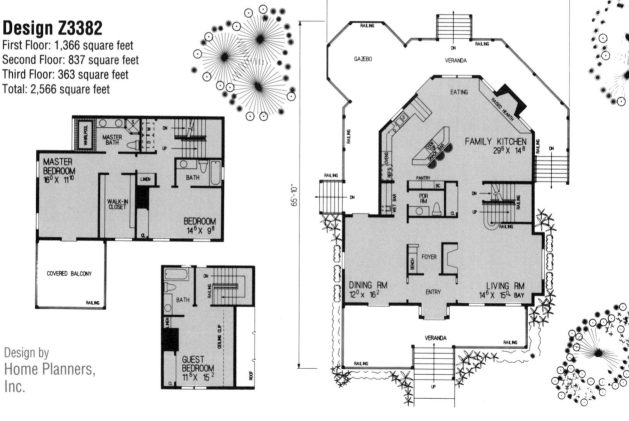

● A simple but charming Queen Anne Victorian, this enchanting three-story home boasts delicately turned rails and decorated columns on its covered front porch. Inside is a floor plan that includes a living room with fireplace and dining room that connects to the kitchen via a wet bar. The adjoining family room contains another fireplace. The second floor holds two bedrooms, one a master suite with grand bath. A tucked-away guest suite on the third floor has a private bath.

Farmhouse & Country Home Plans

No house style better exemplifies family living than the farmhouse. These utilitarian structures portray warmth and security. Rustic, country exteriors conceal cozy interior plans with an abundance of family gathering spots. Covered porches and decks enhance indoor/outdoor relationships and inspire images of Sunday afternoons spent sipping lemonade in the shade.

The typical farmhouse is a two-story home covered with horizontal wood siding, sometimes accented by brick or stone and often featuring dormer windows. Steeply pitched, gabled roofs are covered by wood shingles and feature chimneys appearing at various locations. A covered front porch or wrapping porch is built of simple, square columns and square, dimensioned railings. One-story homes with a country style also appear in this section.

Fireplaces inside highlight great rooms, family rooms and living rooms. Beamed or sloping ceilings provide architectural interest to living areas. Sun rooms and multi-paned windows to the rear brighten the interior and expand livability. Amenity-laden architectural floor planning, plenty of bedrooms and bonus rooms heighten family living.

Design Z9657 provides a rear sun room accessible from the master bedroom, while Design Z9600 features a front-facing sun room to take advantage of south-facing lots. A pleasing floor plan, classic farmhouse facade and just-right square footage make Design Z2774 on page 101 a long-standing favorite. Each of the country or farmhouse designs that follow provides for comfortable family living.

Design Z9657

Square Footage: 2,165

● Step into the sun room from the master
suite, family room or deck in this sunny three-
bedroom country home dressed up with dormers, shutters and bay windows. Along with
formal living and dining rooms, this home also
has a family room flooded with light from a
sliding glass door with arched window above.
The kitchen includes an island and an adjacent
breakfast area. The ample master suite includes
a walk-in closet and a luxurious master bath
with dual lavatories, a shower and a whirlpool
tub. A separate garage is reached via a covered
breezeway across the deck.

Design by
Donald A.
Gardner,
Architect, Inc.

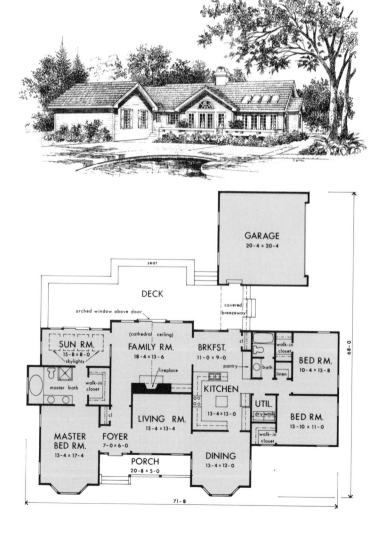

REAR

Design Z9600
Square Footage: 2,053

● This three-bedroom country cottage with sun room at the front takes advantage of south-facing lots. The generous entry foyer allows direct access to the great room, dining room and sun room. A country kitchen with breakfast bar and cooking island provides an abundance of cabinet space. Split away from two family bedrooms is a private master suite with walk-in closets and master bath with whirlpool tub, shower and double-bowl vanity. The great room has direct access to a deck and the sun room. Both the great room and sun room have cathedral ceilings (note skylights in the sun room). A covered breezeway connects the house to the garage. The house is built on a crawlspace foundation.

GARAGE
22-0 × 20-4

covered breezeway

DECK
24-4 × 11-8

seat

down

down

(cathedral ceiling)
GREAT RM
15-4 × 25-4

KIT./BRKFST.
18-8 × 15-8

BED RM.
11-8 × 10-2

walk-in closet

master bath

fireplace

walk-in closets

bath

wash dry

lin.

MASTER
BED RM.
14-8 × 14-2

cl

FOYER
5-0 × 9-8

DINING
13-4 × 12-0

cl

SUN RM.
15-4 × 11-8

optional opening

BED RM.
11-8 × 12-8

skylights

PORCH
18-8 × 5-0

(cathedral ceiling)

down

66-4

67-4

Design by
Donald A.
Gardner,
Architect, Inc.

FRONT

85

Design Z9720
Square Footage: 2,621

● This design provides cottage style in a contemporary floor plan. The heart of this home is the large country kitchen, family room and sun room complex. The breakfast room contains a bay window. Both the family room and living room have fireplaces and built-in cabinets. The master bedroom, sun room and living room open to the spacious deck with spa area. The master suite is a private, sunny retreat off the deck with a luxurious master bath featuring dual lavatories, a garden tub and a separate shower. Two family bedrooms and two full baths are at the opposite end of the house, while a fourth bedroom can function as a study.

Design by
Donald A.
Gardner,
Architect, Inc.

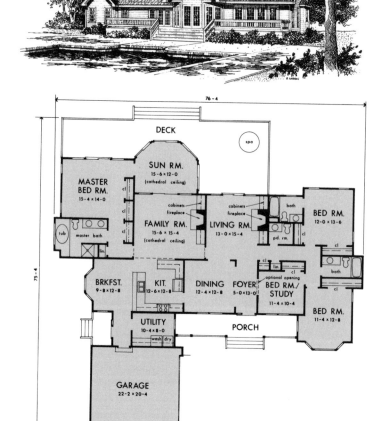

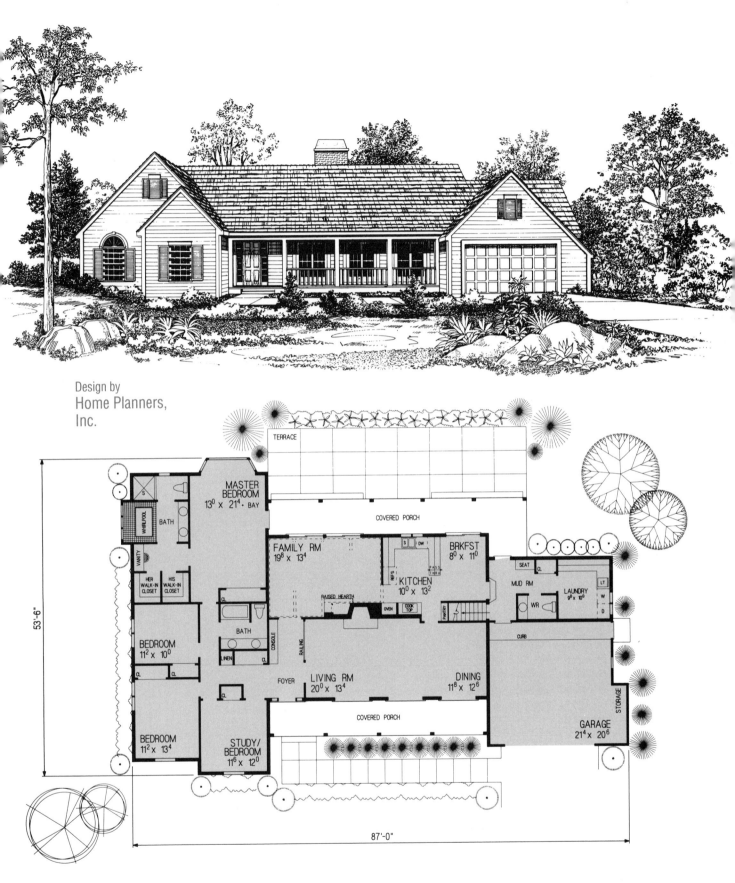

Design by
Home Planners,
Inc.

TERRACE

COVERED PORCH

MASTER
BEDROOM
13⁰ x 21⁴ • BAY

BATH

WHIRLPOOL

VANITY

HER
WALK-IN
CLOSET

HIS
WALK-IN
CLOSET

FAMILY RM
19⁸ x 13⁴

RAISED HEARTH

KITCHEN
10⁰ x 13²

BRKFST
8⁰ x 11⁰

REF'G

PASS THRU

MUD RM

SEAT

LAUNDRY
9⁸ x 10⁰

LT

W

D

WR

BEDROOM
11² x 10⁰

BATH

LINEN

CONSOLE

RAILING

OVEN

COOK TOP

PANTRY

CURB

STORAGE

FOYER

LIVING RM
20⁰ x 13⁴

DINING
11⁸ x 12⁶

BEDROOM
11² x 13⁴

STUDY/
BEDROOM
11⁶ x 12⁰

COVERED PORCH

GARAGE
21⁴ x 20⁶

53'-6"

87'-0"

Design Z3348
Square Footage: 2,549

● Covered porches front and rear will
be the envy of the neighborhood when
this house is built. The interior plan
meets family needs perfectly in well-
zoned areas: a sleeping wing with four
bedrooms and two baths, a living zone
with formal and informal gathering
space, and a work zone with U-shaped
kitchen and laundry with washroom.
The two-car garage has a huge storage
area.

Design Z9707

First Floor: 1,632 square feet
Second Floor: 669 square feet
Total: 2,301 square feet
Bonus Room: 528 square feet

● This open country plan boasts front and rear covered porches and a bonus room for future expansion. The entrance foyer with sloped ceiling has a Palladian window clerestory to allow natural light in. The spacious great room has a fireplace, cathedral ceiling and clerestory with arched windows. A second-floor balcony overlooks the great room. A U-shaped kitchen provides the ideal layout for food preparation. For flexibility, access is provided to the bonus room from both the first and second floors. The first-floor master bedroom features a bath with dual lavatories, separate tub and shower and a walk-in closet. Two large bedrooms and a full bath are located on the second floor. The plan is available with a crawl-space foundation.

Design by
Donald A.
Gardner,
Architect, Inc.

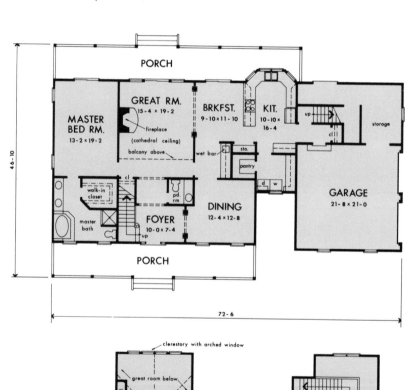

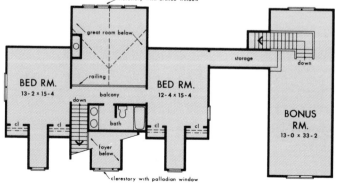

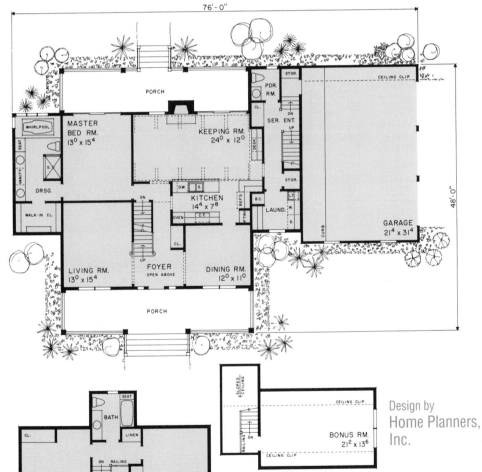

Design Z3566

First Floor: 1,635 square feet
Second Floor: 586 square feet
Total: 2,221 square feet
Bonus Room: 321 square feet

● Don't be fooled by the humble appearance of this farmhouse. All the amenities abound. Covered porches are located to both the front and rear of the home. A grand front entrance opens into living and dining rooms. The family will surely enjoy the ambience of the keeping room with its fireplace and beamed ceiling. A service entry, with laundry nearby, separates the garage from the main house. An over-the-garage bonus room allows for room to grow or a nice study. Two quaint bedrooms and full bath make up the second floor. Each bedroom features a lovely dormer window.

Design by
Home Planners, Inc.

Design Z9701

First Floor: 1,720 square feet
Second Floor: 652 square feet
Total: 2,372 square feet
Bonus room: 553 square feet

● This elegant country home, with both front and rear porches, offers a pleasing appearance with its variety of materials and refined detailing. The open floor plan is reinforced by the vaulted great room and entrance foyer with clerestory windows in dormers above. Both spaces are open to a balcony/loft area above. The master suite with cathedral ceiling and large walk-in closet is located on the first floor for privacy and accessibility. Nine-foot ceilings grace much of the first floor. The second floor, with its eight-foot ceilings, has two large bedrooms, a full bath and a bonus room over the garage with space available for another bath. The plan is available with a crawl-space foundation.

Design by
Donald A.
Gardner,
Architect, Inc.

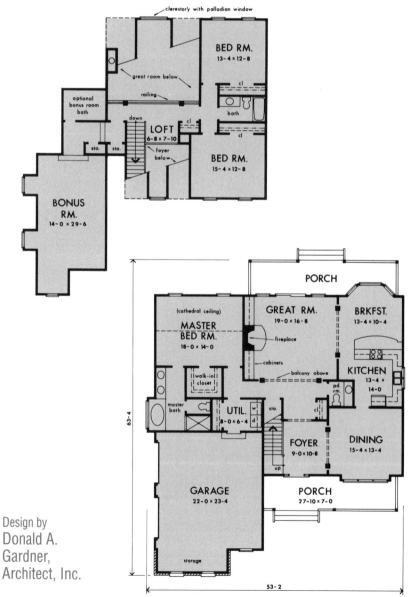

90

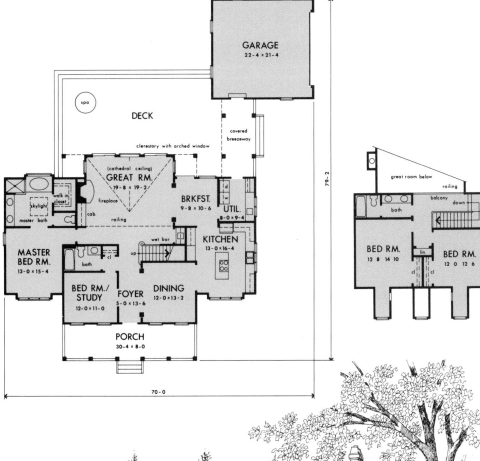

GARAGE
22-4 × 21-4

spa

DECK

clerestory with arched window

covered breezeway

79-2

(cathedral ceiling)
GREAT RM.
19-8 × 19-2

fireplace

railing

BRKFST.
9-8 × 10-6

UTIL.
8-0 × 9-4

walk in closet

skylight

master bath

cab.

wet bar

KITCHEN
13-0 × 16-4

MASTER
BED RM.
13-0 × 15-4

bath

cl

up

BED RM./
STUDY
12-0 × 11-0

FOYER
5-0 × 13-6

DINING
12-0 × 13-2

PORCH
30-4 × 8-0

70-0

great room below

balcony

bath

down

railing

BED RM.
12 8 14 10

lin.

cl

cl

BED RM.
12 0 12 6

Design Z9703

First Floor: 1,783 square feet
Second Floor: 611 square feet
Total: 2,394 square feet

● Onlookers will delight in the symmetry of this facade's arched windows and dormers. The interior offers a great room with cathedral ceiling. Other first-floor spaces have 9' ceilings while second-floor spaces feature 8½' ceilings. This open plan is also packed with the latest design features including a kitchen with large island, wet bar, bedroom/study combo on first floor and gorgeous master suite with master bath consisting of double-bowl vanity, shower, whirlpool tub, large walk-in closet, separate commode compartment and skylight. An expansive rear deck and generous covered front porch offer maximum outdoor livability. The plan is available with crawl-space foundation.

Design by
Donald A.
Gardner,
Architect, Inc.

Design Z9668

First Floor: 1,254 square feet
Second Floor: 1,060 square feet
Total: 2,314 square feet

Design by
Donald A.
Gardner,
Architect, Inc.

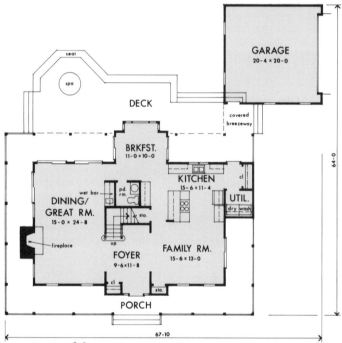

● This stylish country farmhouse shows off its good looks both front and rear. A wraparound porch allows sheltered access to all first-level areas along with a covered breezeway to the garage. On the first floor, the spacious, open layout has all the latest features. The master bedroom on the second level has a fireplace, large walk-in closet and a master bath with shower, whirlpool tub and double-bowl vanity. Three additional bedrooms share a full bath with double-bowl vanity.

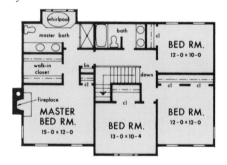

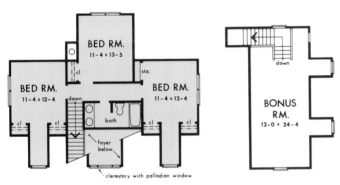

BED RM.
11-4 x 13-5

BED RM.
11-4 x 12-4

BED RM.
11-4 x 12-4

sto.

cl

cl

cl

cl

down

bath

foyer
below

clerestory with palladian window

BONUS
RM.
12-0 x 24-4

down

Design Z9706

First Floor: 1,585 square feet
Second Floor: 731 square feet
Total: 2,316 square feet
Bonus Room: 401 square feet

● This complete farmhouse projects an exciting and comfortable feeling with its wraparound porch, arched windows and dormers. A Palladian window in the clerestory above the entrance foyer allows an abundance of natural light. The large kitchen, with carefully planned layout incorporating a cooking island, easily services the breakfast area and dining room. The generous great room with fireplace is accessible to the spacious screened porch for mosquito-free outside living. The master bedroom suite, located on the first level for privacy and convenience, has a luxurious master bath. The second level allows for three bedrooms and a full bath. Don't miss the garage with bonus room—both meet the main house via a covered breezeway. The plan is available with a crawl-space foundation.

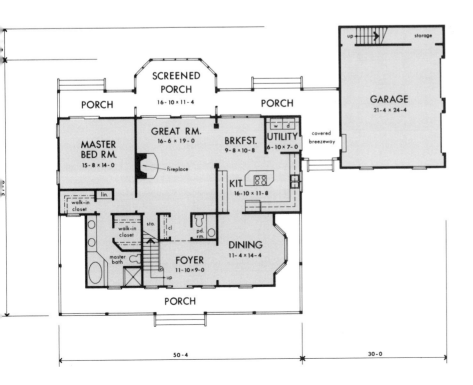

SCREENED
PORCH
16-10 x 11-4

PORCH

PORCH

GARAGE
21-4 x 24-4

up

storage

MASTER
BED RM.
15-8 x 14-0

GREAT RM.
16-6 x 19-0

fireplace

BRKFST.
9-8 x 10-8

UTILITY
6-10 x 7-0

w d

covered
breezeway

walk-in
closet

lin.

walk-in
closet

sta.

cl

KIT.
16-10 x 11-8

pd.
rm.

DINING
11-4 x 14-4

master
bath

FOYER
11-10 x 9-0

up

PORCH

50-4

30-0

Design by
**Donald A.
Gardner,
Architect, Inc.**

Design Z9677

First Floor: 1,584 square feet
Second Floor: 867 square feet
Total: 2,451 square feet

● Flexibility is the key to the appeal of this country-style plan. The dining room/great room can be built as one great room with the dining room relocated to the family room. The master suite has a large walk-in closet, a fireplace and a master bath with shower, whirlpool tub and double-bowl vanity. Both the sun room and master bath have access to a uniquely shaped deck. Note that there is space available on the deck for a hot tub. The screened porch offers the best in outdoor living space. Three bedrooms on the second level are joined by two full baths for convenience. Dormer windows on the second floor project out from two of the bedrooms, allowing room for window seats or storage.

Design by
Donald A.
Gardner,
Architect, Inc.

BED RM.
11-10 x 11-4

BED RM.
13-0 x 12-0

BED RM.
13-4 x 12-0

DECK

SUN RM.
15-4 x 9-6

wet bar

pd. rm.

KITCHEN
13-4 x 13-8

spa

seat

whirlpool

master bath

walk-in closet

MASTER BED RM.
15-0 x 14-4

fireplace

fireplace

DINING/
GREAT RM.
15-4 x 23-8

FAMILY RM.
13-4 x 14-4

breakfast bar

SCREENED PORCH
10-4 x 16-0

storage

storage

GARAGE
21-8 x 21-0

PORCH
33-6 x 7-0

41-4

90-2

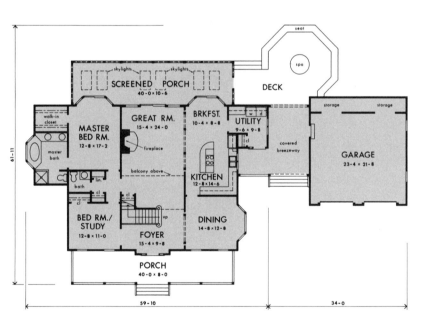

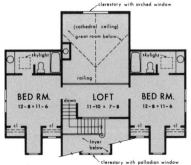

Design Z9712

First Floor: 1,766 square feet
Second Floor: 670 square feet
Total: 2,436 square feet

● With a casually elegant exterior, this four-bedroom farmhouse celebrates sunlight with a Palladian window dormer, skylit screened porch and rear arched window. The clerestory window in the two-story foyer throws natural light across the loft to the great room with fireplace and cathedral ceiling. The center island kitchen and breakfast area open to the great room through an elegant colonnade. The first-floor master suite is a calm retreat opening to the screened porch through a bay area. A garden tub, dual lavatories and a separate shower are touches of luxury in the master bath. The second floor provides two bedrooms with private baths and a loft area.

Design by
Donald A.
Gardner,
Architect, Inc.

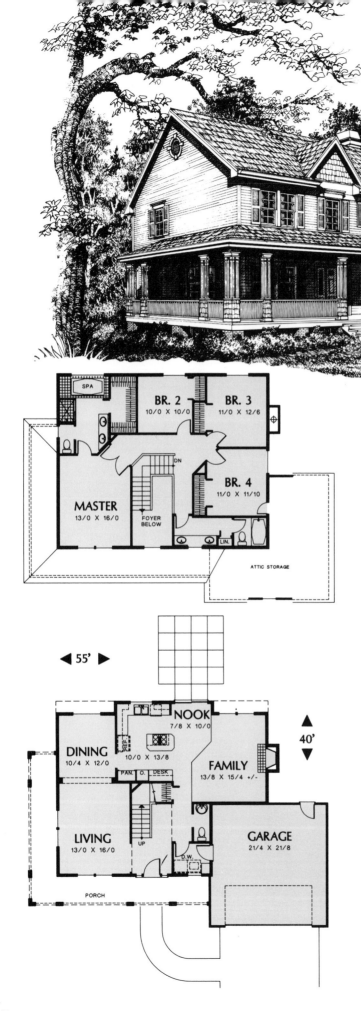

Design by
Alan Mascord
Design Associates, Inc.

Floor Plan Labels

Second Floor:
- SPA
- BR. 2 — 10/0 X 10/0
- BR. 3 — 11/0 X 12/6
- BR. 4 — 11/0 X 11/10
- MASTER — 13/0 X 16/0
- DN
- FOYER BELOW
- LIN.
- ATTIC STORAGE

First Floor:
- ◄ 55' ►
- ▲ 40' ▼
- NOOK — 7/8 X 10/0
- DINING — 10/4 X 12/0
- REF.
- 10/0 X 13/8
- FAMILY — 13/8 X 15/4 +/-
- PAN. O. DESK
- LIVING — 13/0 X 16/0
- UP
- D.W.
- GARAGE — 21/4 X 21/8
- PORCH

Design Z9497

First Floor: 1,037 square feet
Second Floor: 1,090 square feet
Total: 2,127 square feet

● Cedar siding makes a beautiful difference in this two-story country plan. Its symmetrical floor plan serves the needs of family living. Main living areas radiate from the entry hall: the formal living room is to the left and connects directly to the dining room; the family room is to the right and behind the garage. An L-shaped kitchen includes an island cooktop and a casual eating area that contains sliding glass doors to a rear terrace. The bedrooms are on the second floor and center around the open-railed staircase. The master bedroom contains a gigantic walk-in closet and a whirlpool tub and separate shower. Family bedrooms share a full bath with double-sink vanity.

Design Z9235

First Floor: 919 square feet
Second Floor: 927 square feet
Total: 1,846 square feet

● Wonderful country design begins with the wraparound porch of this plan. Explore further and find a two-story entry with a coat closet and plant shelf above and a strategically placed staircase alongside. The island kitchen with a boxed window over the sink is adjacent to a large bay-windowed dinette. The great room includes many windows and a fireplace. A powder bath and laundry room are both conveniently placed on the first floor. Upstairs, the large master suite contains His and Hers walk-in closets, corner windows and a bath area featuring a double vanity and whirlpool tub. Two pleasant secondary bedrooms have interesting angles and a third bedroom in the front features a volume ceiling and arched window.

© 1989 design basics inc.

Design by
Design
Basics,
Inc.

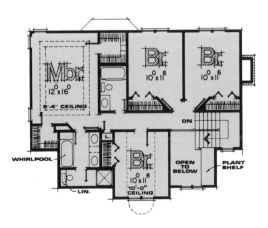

Design Z9242

First Floor: 1,322 square feet
Second Floor: 1,272 square feet
Total: 2,594 square feet

● Here's the luxury you've been looking for—from the wraparound covered front porch to the bright sun room at the rear off the breakfast room. A sunken family room with fireplace serves everyday casual gatherings, while the more formal living and dining rooms are reserved for special entertaining situations. The kitchen has a central island with snack bar and is located most conveniently for serving and cleaning up. Upstairs are four bedrooms, one a lovely master suite with French doors into the master bath and a whirlpool tub in a dramatic bay window. A double vanity in the shared bath easily serves the three family bedrooms.

Design by
Design
Basics,
Inc.

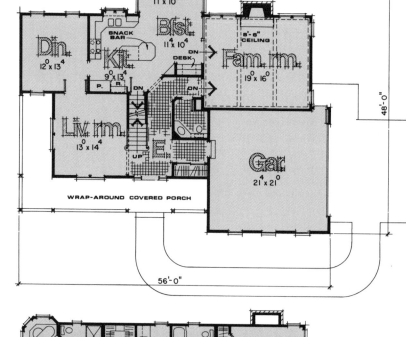

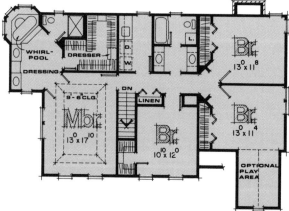

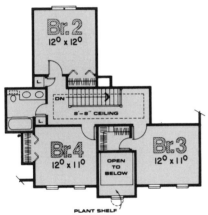

Br. 2
12⁰ x 12⁰

DN

9'-8" CEILING

Br. 4
12⁰ x 11⁰

OPEN
TO
BELOW

Br. 3
12⁰ x 11⁰

PLANT SHELF

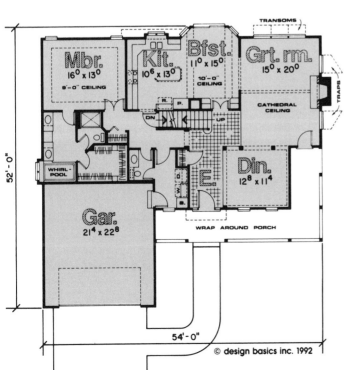

Mbr.
16⁰ x 13⁰

9'-0" CEILING

Kit.
10⁶ x 13⁰

Bfst.
11⁰ x 15⁰

10'-0"
CEILING

Grt. rm.
15⁰ x 20⁰

CATHEDRAL
CEILING

TRANSOMS

DN

R. P.

UP

WHIRL-
POOL

Din.
12⁸ x 11⁴

Gar.
21⁴ x 22⁸

WRAP AROUND PORCH

52'-0"

54'-0"

© design basics inc. 1992

Design Z9387

First Floor: 1,570 square feet
Second Floor: 707 square feet
Total: 2,277 square feet

● A wraparound, covered porch and bright windows create a striking front elevation. The entry offers a tremendous open view of the dining and great rooms. A fireplace centers on the cathedral ceiling which soars to over 16 feet high in the great room. French doors to the dinette add a formal touch. The kitchen includes a Lazy Susan, a large food-preparation island and an ample pantry. Double doors access the first-floor master bedroom with boxed ceiling. The master bath features a large whirlpool, dual lavatories, a makeup vanity and a walk-in closet. Three family bedrooms are on the second floor.

Design by
Design
Basics,
Inc.

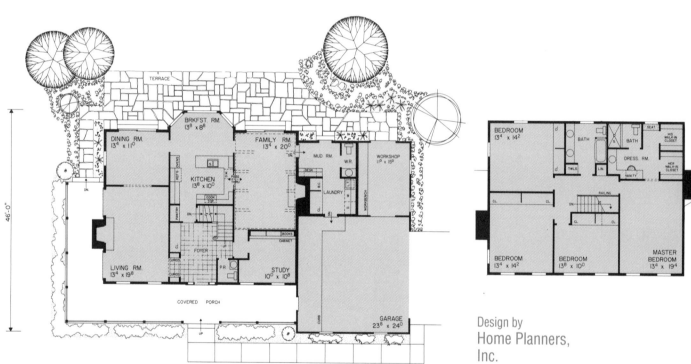

Design by
Home Planners,
Inc.

Design Z2946 First Floor: 1,590 square feet
Second Floor: 1,344 square feet; Total: 2,934 square feet

● Here's a traditional design that's made for down-home hospitality, the pleasures of casual conversation, and the good grace of pleasant company. The star attractions are the large covered porch and terrace, perfectly relaxing gathering points for family and

friends. Inside, though, the design is truly a hard worker; separate living room and family room, each with its own fireplace; formal dining room; large kitchen and breakfast area with bay windows; separate study; workshop with plenty of room to ma-

neuver; mud room; and four bedrooms up, including a master suite. Not to be overlooked are the curio niches, the powder room, the built in bookshelves, the kitchen pass-through, and pantry. For information on customizing the design, call 1-800-322-6797, ext. 800.

Design Z2774

First Floor: 1,370 square feet
Second Floor: 969 square feet
Total: 2,339 square feet

● Another Farmhouse adaptation with all the most up-to-date features expected in a new home. Beginning with the formal areas, this design offers pleasures for the entire family. There is the quiet corner living room which has an opening to the sizable dining room. This room will enjoy plenty of natural light from the delightful bay window overlooking the rear yard. It is also conveniently located with the efficient U-shaped kitchen just a step away. The kitchen features many built-ins with pass-thru to the beamed ceiling breakfast room. Sliding glass doors to the terrace are fine attractions in both the sunken family room and breakfast room. The service entrance to the garage is flanked by a clothes closet and a large, walk-in pantry. There is a secondary entrance thru the laundry room. Recreational activities and hobbies can be pursued in the basement area. Four bedrooms, two baths upstairs. For information on customizing this design, call 1-800-332-6797, ext. 800.

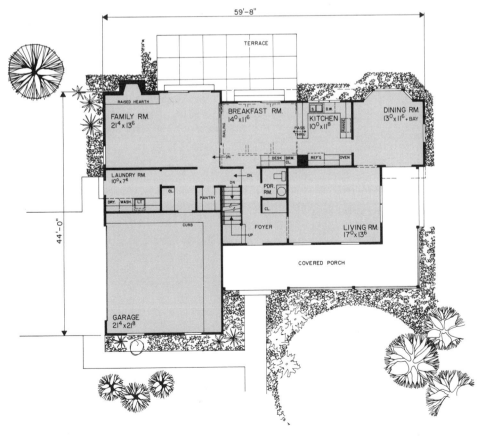

Design by
Home Planners,
Inc.

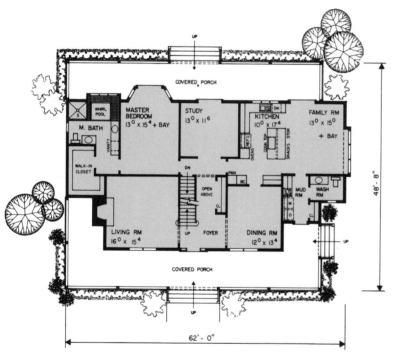

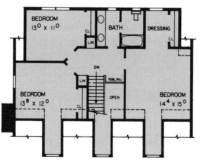

Design Z3396

First Floor: 1,829 square feet
Second Floor: 947 square feet
Total: 2,776 square feet

● Rustic charm abounds in this pleasant farm-house rendition. Covered porches to the front and rear enclose living potential for the whole family. Flanking the entrance foyer are the living and dining rooms. To the rear is the L-shaped kitchen with island cook top and snack bar. A small family room/breakfast nook is attached. A private study is tucked away on this floor next to the master suite. On the second floor are three bedrooms and a full bath. Two of the bedrooms have charming dormer windows.

Design by
Home Planners,
Inc.

Design by
Home Planners,
Inc.

Design by
Home Planners,
Inc.

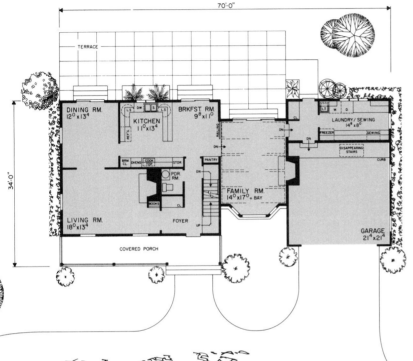

Design Z2908

First Floor: 1,427 square feet
Second Floor: 1,153 square feet
Total: 2,580 square feet

● This Early American farmhouse offers plenty of modern comfort with its covered front porch with pillars and rails, double chimneys, building attachment, and four upstairs bedrooms. The first floor attachment includes a family room with bay window. It leads from the main house to a two-car garage. The family room certainly is the central focus of this fine design, with its own fireplace and rear entrance to a laundry and sewing room behind the garage. Disappearing stairs in the building attachment lead to attic space over the garage. The upstairs also is accessible from stairs just off the front foyer. Included is a master bedroom suite. Downstairs one finds a modern kitchen with breakfast room, dining room, and front living room. For information on customizing this design, call 1-800-332-6797, ext. 800.

Design Z9001

First Floor: 1,308 square feet
Second Floor: 751 square feet
Total: 2,059 square feet

● A wraparound veranda and simple, uncluttered lines give this home an unassuming elegance that is characteristic of its farmhouse heritage. The kitchen overlooks an octagon-shaped breakfast room with full-length windows. The master bedroom features plenty of closet space and an elegant bath. Located within an oversized bay window is a garden tub with adjacent planter and glass-enclosed shower. Upstairs, two bedrooms share a bath with separate dressing and bathing areas. The balcony sitting area is perfect as a playroom or study. Plans for a detached two-car garage are included.

Design by
Larry W.
Garnett &
Associates, Inc.

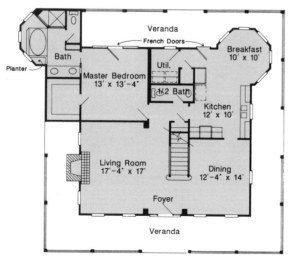

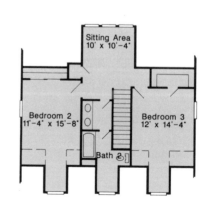

Width 53'
Depth 45' - 4"

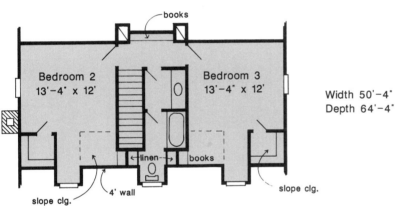

books

Bedroom 2
13'-4" x 12'

Bedroom 3
13'-4" x 12'

linen

books

slope clg.

4' wall

slope clg.

Design by
Larry W.
Garnett &
Associates, Inc.

Design Z9121

First Floor: 1,266 square feet
Second Floor: 639 square feet
Total: 1,905 square feet

● Complete with dormers and a covered
front porch, the facade details of this home
are repeated at the side-loaded garage, making it a perfectly charming plan from any
angle. From the raised foyer, step down into
the living room with fireplace. This area
opens to a dining room which has a French
door to the rear yard. Close by is a kitchen
with pantry and access to a utility room and
the garage. The master suite is on the first
floor for convenience. Note the two large
walk-in closets here. Upstairs there are two
secondary bedrooms and a full compartmented bath. An entry near the garage contains a
staircase to an optional storage room. This
space could be developed later as a mother-
in-law suite or home office.

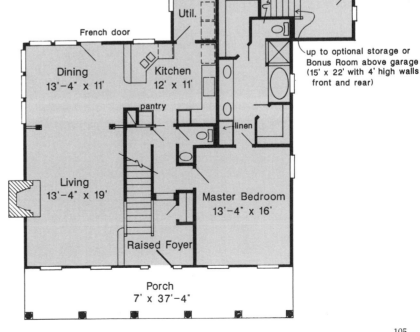

Width 50'-4"
Depth 64'-4"

2-Car Garage
21'-4" x 19'-4"

Util.

French door

up to optional storage or
Bonus Room above garage
(15' x 22' with 4' high walls
front and rear)

Dining
13'-4" x 11'

Kitchen
12' x 11'

pantry

linen

Living
13'-4" x 19'

Master Bedroom
13'-4" x 16'

Raised Foyer

Porch
7' x 37'-4"

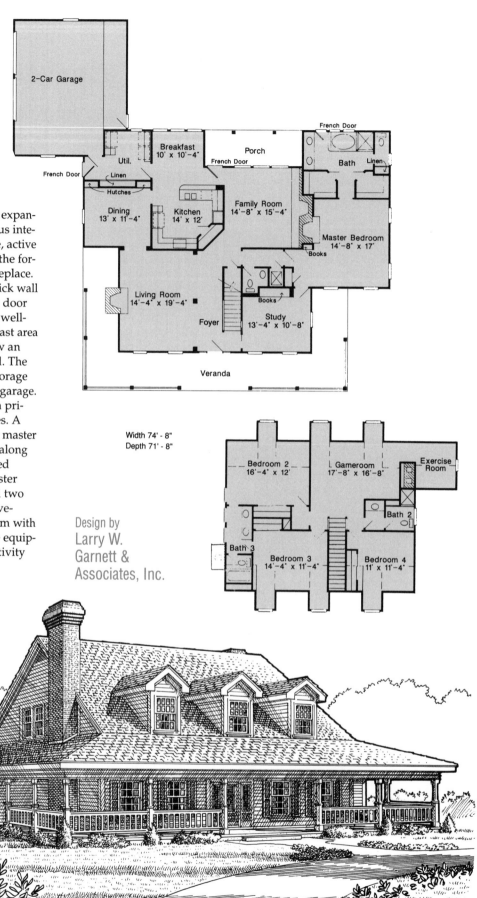

Design Z9004

First Floor: 2,166 square feet
Second Floor: 1,169 square feet
Total: 3,335 square feet

● This farmhouse design, with its expansive wraparound porch and spacious interior, will suit the needs of any large, active family. The foyer opens directly to the formal living room with an elegant fireplace. The family room offers a unique brick wall with built-in fireplace and a French door opening onto a covered porch. The well-planned kitchen overlooks a breakfast area with full-length windows that allow an uninterrupted view of the rear yard. The large utility room, with plenty of storage space, leads to an attached two-car garage. The master bedroom has access to a private study with built-in bookshelves. A third fireplace further enhances the master area. His and Hers walk-in closets, along with a garden tub and glass-enclosed shower, complete this secluded master suite. Upstairs, three bedrooms and two baths offer plenty of space and convenience for the children. A game room with an alcove that is perfect for exercise equipment provides a versatile family activity area.

Design by
Larry W.
Garnett &
Associates, Inc.

2-Car Garage

Breakfast
10' x 10'-4"

Porch
French Door

Util.

Linen

Bath

Linen

French Door

Hutches

Dining
13' x 11'-4"

Kitchen
14' x 12'

Family Room
14'-8" x 15'-4"

Master Bedroom
14'-8" x 17'

Books

Living Room
14'-4" x 19'-4"

Books

Foyer

Study
13'-4" x 10'-8"

Veranda

French Door

Width 74' - 8"
Depth 71' - 8"

Bedroom 2
16'-4" x 12'

Gameroom
17'-8" x 16'-8"

Exercise
Room

Bath 2

Bath 3

Bedroom 3
14'-4" x 11'-4"

Bedroom 4
11' x 11'-4"

Design Z9005

First Floor: 1,995 square feet
Second Floor: 1,077 square feet
Total: 3,072 square feet

● A wraparound front porch and dormer windows give this home a casual and comfortable appearance. A leaded-glass transom above the front door, along with the dormer window in the sloped ceiling, fill the foyer with natural light. The large living area features French doors on each side of an elegant fireplace, and a built-in wet bar. An island cooktop, along with a walk-in pantry are part of the well-planned kitchen. The utility room, with extra work space, leads to an attached two-car garage and storage area. The master bedroom has generous closet space and a two-way fireplace opening into the master bath. His and Hers lavatories, an oversized tub and glass-enclosed shower complete this elegant master bath. The balcony has French doors opening into a large game room. Bedroom 3 has a private bath, while Bedroom 2 shares access to a bath with the game room. Each bedroom has a sloped ceiling and a cozy alcove created by the dormer window.

Design by
Larry W.
Garnett &
Associates, Inc.

Width 79'
Depth 60' - 6"

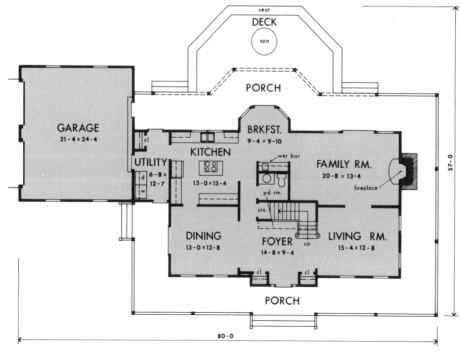

Design by
Donald A.
Gardner,
Architect, Inc.

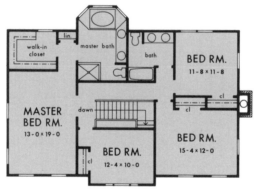

master bath

lin.

walk-in closet

bath

BED RM.
11-8 × 11-8

cl

MASTER BED RM.
13-0 × 19-0

down

cl

BED RM.
15-4 × 12-0

BED RM.
12-4 × 10-0

cl

seat

DECK

spa

PORCH

GARAGE
21-4 × 24-4

cl

BRKFST.
9-4 × 9-10

KITCHEN
13-0 × 13-4

wet bar

FAMILY RM.
20-8 × 13-4

fireplace

UTILITY
6-8 × 12-7

d
w

pd. rm.

sto.

57-0

DINING
13-0 × 12-8

FOYER
14-8 × 9-4

up

LIVING RM.
15-4 × 12-8

cl

cl

PORCH

80-0

Design Z9667
First Floor: 1,357 square feet
Second Floor: 1,204 square feet
Total: 2,561 square feet

● This grand four-bedroom farmhouse with wraparound porch has eye-catching features: a double-gabled roof, Palladian window at the upper level, arched window on the lower level and intricately detailed brick chimney. Entry to the home reveals a generous foyer with direct access to all areas. The living room opens to the foyer and provides a formal entertaining area. The exceptionally large family room allows for more casual living. Look for a fireplace, wet bar and direct access to a porch and deck here. The lavish kitchen boasts a cooking island and serves the dining room, breakfast and deck areas. The master suite on the second level has a large walk-in closet and master bath with a whirlpool tub, shower and double-bowl vanity. Three additional bedrooms share a full bath.

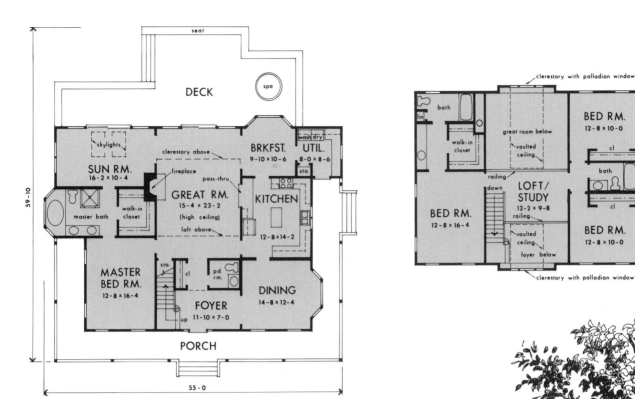

DECK

seat

spa

SUN RM.
16-2 × 10-4

skylights

clerestory above

BRKFST.
9-10 × 10-6

UTIL.
8-0 × 8-6

wash dry

sto.

master bath

walk-in closet

fireplace

pass-thru

GREAT RM.
15-4 × 23-2
(high ceiling)

loft above

KITCHEN

12-8 × 14-2

MASTER BED RM.
12-8 × 16-4

sto.

cl

pd. rm.

FOYER
11-10 × 7-0

up

DINING
14-8 × 12-4

PORCH

55-0

59-10

bath

lin

walk-in closet

great room below

vaulted ceiling

railing

BED RM.
12-8 × 10-0

cl

bath

cl

clerestory with palladian window

BED RM.
12-8 × 16-4

down

LOFT/
STUDY
12-2 × 9-8

railing

vaulted ceiling

foyer below

BED RM.
12-8 × 10-0

clerestory with palladian window

Design Z9616

First Floor: 1,734 square feet
Second Floor: 958 square feet
Total: 2,692 square feet

● A wraparound covered porch at the front and sides of this home and the open deck with spa and seating provide plenty of outside living area. A central great room features a vaulted ceiling, fireplace and clerestory windows above. The loft/study on the second floor overlooks this gathering area. Besides a formal dining room, kitchen, breakfast room and sun room on the first floor, there is also a generous master suite with garden tub. Three second-floor bedrooms complete sleeping accommodations. The plan includes a crawl-space foundation.

Design by
Donald A.
Gardner,
Architect, Inc.

FRONT

REAR

Design Z9708

First Floor: 2,238 square feet
Second Floor: 768 square feet
Total: 3,006 square feet

● This grand country farmhouse with wraparound porch offers comfortable living at its finest. The open floor plan is reinforced by a vaulted great room and entrance foyer with Palladian clerestory windows in dormers above. All spaces are generous in size with nine-foot ceilings on the first level and eight-foot ceilings on the second. The master suite has beautiful bay windows and a well-designed master bath with cathedral ceiling, His and Hers vanities, shower, whirlpool tub and spacious walk-in closet. The second level has two large bedrooms, a full bath and plenty of attic storage. The plan is available with a crawl-space foundation.

Design by
Donald A.
Gardner,
Architect, Inc.

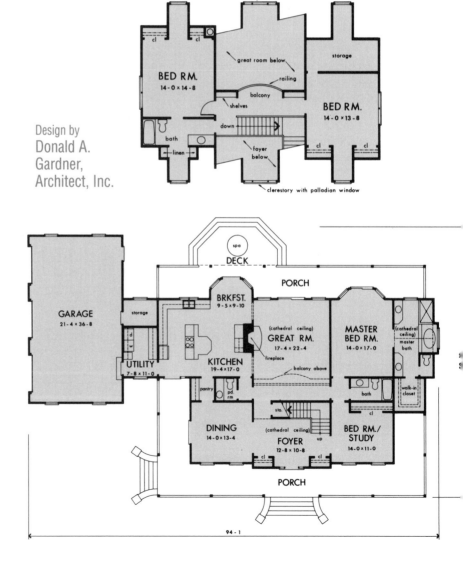

French & European Designs

A warm, welcoming look characterizes French and European designs. From the formal symmetry of French design to the asymmetrical projections of European style, these homes have graceful, elegant appearances.

Although French style is architecturally diverse, most contemporary French houses share several key features. French style is defined by hipped roofs, symmetrical facades, brick exteriors, corner quoins, arched windows and dentils. Hipped roofs range from moderately pitched roofs to the mansard roof, a two-pitched hipped version with a steep lower slope, created by 17th-Century architect Francois Mansart.

French architectural detailing is borrowed from Georgian design, including quoins (stone or brick sections used to accentuate the corner of a house), and dentils, which are toothy decorations along the cornice.

European homes present a stucco and stone facade, multi-level, hipped roof lines or gabled roofs and arched windows and entryways.

Design Z2779 on page 114 is an impressive French home with a hipped roof, a symmetrical facade and an equally appealing interior. For an exquisite example of European style, see Design Z9871 on page 122.

Design Z3559
Square Footage: 2,916

● Intricate details make the most of
this lovely one-story: high, varied
roofline, circle and half-circle window
detailing, multi-paned windows, and
a solid chimney stack. The floor plan
caters to comfortable living. Besides
the living room/dining room area to
the rear, there is a large conversation
area with fireplace and plenty of windows. The kitchen is separated from
living areas by an angled snack bar
counter. A media room to the front of
the plan provides space for more private activities. Three bedrooms grace
the right side of the plan. The master
suite features a tray vaulted ceiling
and sliding glass doors to the rear terrace. The dressing area is graced by
His and Hers walk-in closets, double-
bowl lavatory, and compartmented
commode. The shower area is highlighted with glass block and is sunken
down one step. A garden whirlpool
finishes off the area.

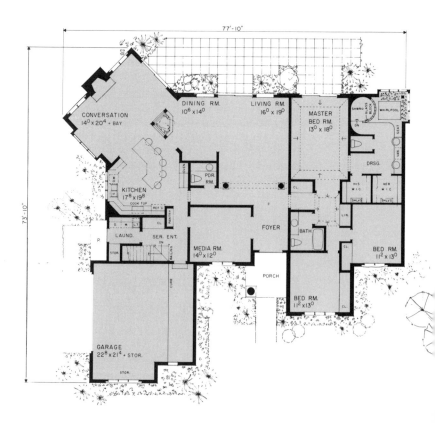

Design by
Home Planners,
Inc.

112

Design Z3558 First Floor: 2,328 square feet; Second Floor: 603 square feet; Total: 2,931 square feet

● This home will keep even the most active family from feeling cramped. A broad foyer opens to a living room that measures 24 feet across and features sliding glass doors to a rear terrace and a covered porch. Adjacent to the kitchen is a conversation area with additional access to the covered porch, a snack bar, fireplace and a window bay. A butler's pantry leads to the formal dining room. Placed conveniently on the first floor, the master suite features a roomy bath with a huge walk-in closet and dual vanities. Two large bedrooms are found on the second floor.

Design by
Home Planners,
Inc.

Design Z2779
Square Footage: 3,225

● This French design is surely impressive. The exterior appearance will brighten any area with its French roof, paned-glass windows, masonry brick privacy wall and double front doors. The inside is just as appealing. Note the unique placement of rooms and features. The entry hall is large and leads to each of the areas in this plan. The formal dining room is outstanding and guests can enter through the entry hall. While serving one can enter by way of the butler's pantry (notice its size and that it has a sink). To the right of the entry is a sizable parlor. Then there is the gathering room with fireplace, sliding glass doors and adjacent study. The work center is also outstanding. There is the U-shaped kitchen, island range, snack bar, breakfast nook, pantry plus washroom and large laundry near service entrance. Basement stairs are also nearby.

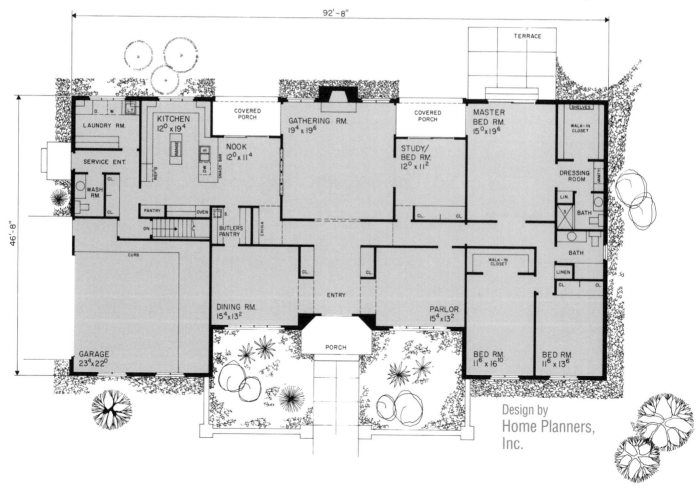

Design by
Home Planners, Inc.

Design Z3368
Square Footage: 2,722

● Roof lines are the key to the interesting exterior of this design. Their configuration allows for sloped ceilings in the gathering room and large foyer. The master bedroom suite has a huge walk-in closet, garden whirlpool and separate shower. Two family bedrooms share a full bath. One of these bedrooms could be used as a media room with pass-through wet bar. Note the large kitchen with conversation bay and the wide terrace to the rear.

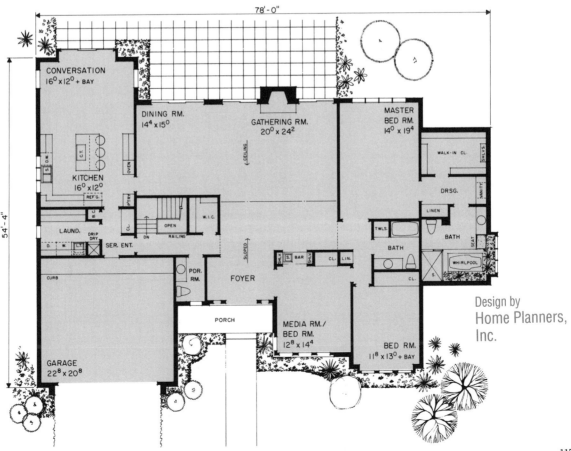

Design by
Home Planners, Inc.

Design Z9323

Square Footage: 2,276

● Drama and harmony are expressed through the use of a variety of elegant exterior materials. An expansive entry views the private den with French doors and an open dining room (both rooms have 10-foot, 8-inch ceilings). The great room with a window-framed fireplace is conveniently located next to the kitchen/bayed breakfast area. Special amenities include a wet bar/servery, two pantries, planning desk, and snack bar. Two secluded secondary bedrooms enjoy easy access to a compartmented bath with two lavs. His and Hers closets and a built-in entertainment center grace the master bedroom. A luxurious master bath features glass blocks over the whirlpool, double lavs and an extra linen storage cabinet. An alternate elevation is provided at no extra cost.

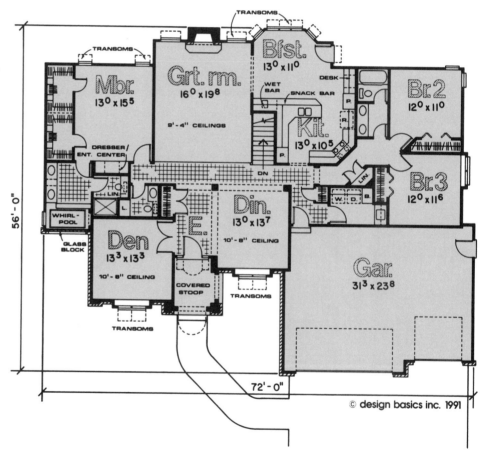

© design basics inc. 1991

Design by
Design
Basics,
Inc.

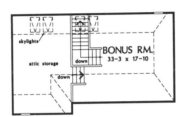

skylights

attic storage

BONUS RM.
33-3 x 17-10

down

down

Design Z9709

Square Footage: 2,663
Bonus Room: 653 square feet

● This stately one-story home displays large arched windows, round columns, a covered porch, and brick veneer siding. The arched window in the clerestory above the entrance provides natural light to the interior. The great room boasts a cathedral ceiling, a fireplace, built-in cabinets, and bookshelves. Sliding glass doors lead to the sun room. The L-shaped kitchen services the dining room, the breakfast area and the great room. The master bedroom suite, with a fireplace, uses private passage to the deck and its spa. Three additional bedrooms—one could serve as a study—are at the other end of the house for privacy. This plan is available with a crawl-space foundation.

Design by
Donald A.
Gardner,
Architect, Inc.

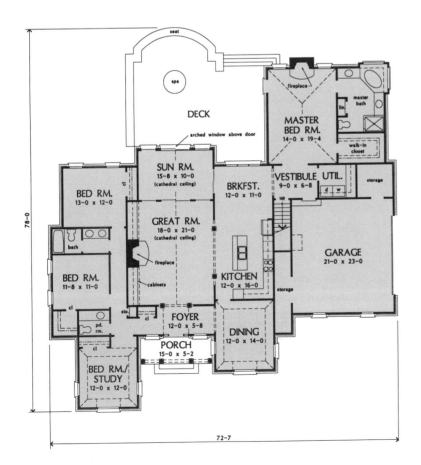

seat

spa

DECK

arched window above door

fireplace

MASTER BED RM.
14-0 x 19-4

master bath

lin.

walk-in closet

SUN RM.
15-8 x 10-0
(cathedral ceiling)

BRKFST.
12-0 x 11-0

VESTIBULE UTIL.
9-0 x 6-8

storage

d w

up

BED RM.
13-0 x 12-0

cl

GREAT RM.
18-0 x 21-0
(cathedral ceiling)

bath

fireplace

cabinets

KITCHEN
12-0 x 16-0

GARAGE
21-0 x 23-0

storage

BED RM.
11-8 x 11-0

cl

pd. rm.

sto.

cl

FOYER
12-0 x 5-8

DINING
12-0 x 14-0

cl

PORCH
15-0 x 5-2

BED RM./STUDY
12-0 x 12-0

78-0

72-7

B. NATHAN.

Design Z9130

Square Footage: 2,349
Bonus Room: 398 square feet

● Brick arches at the angled front entry along with multiple gables and a bay window give the exterior of this home a comfortable, yet distinctive look. Unique details set this plan apart: angled living room with 10-foot ceiling, fireplace in the master bedroom, octagonal breakfast room. The kitchen features an island and pass-through bar to the breakfast room. The rear covered porch can be accessed through two sets of French doors. Additional space above the garage can be developed as needed for live-in relatives, a college student or for studio or hobby space. There's also convenient storage space in the garage.

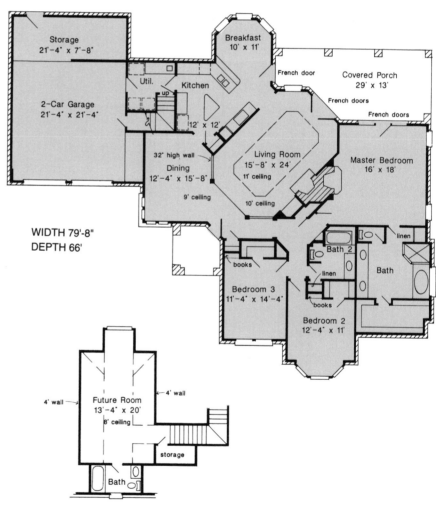

WIDTH 79'-8"
DEPTH 66'

Design by
Larry W.
Garnett &
Associates, Inc.

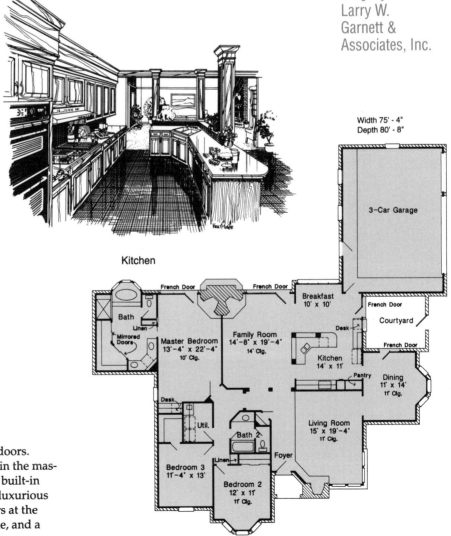

Design by
Larry W.
Garnett &
Associates, Inc.

Design Z9025

Square Footage: 2,481

● Multiple gables, bay windows and corner windows with transoms above provide an exterior reminiscent of English countryside homes. A marble floor in the foyer extends into the living room as an elegant fireplace hearth. The formal dining room features an eleven-foot ceiling, bay window, and French doors that open onto a private dining terrace. A spacious kitchen overlooks the breakfast area and the family room which has a corner fireplace and dramatic fourteen-foot ceiling with transom windows above triple French doors. Another corner fireplace is located in the master bedroom, which also contains a built-in desk and triple French doors. The luxurious master bath features mirrored doors at the large walk-in closet, a dressing table, and a whirlpool tub inset in a bay window.

Kitchen

Width 75' - 4"
Depth 80' - 8"

3-Car Garage

French Door

French Door

Breakfast
10' x 10'

French Door

Courtyard

French Door

Bath

Linen

Mirrored
Doors

Master Bedroom
13'-4" x 22'-4"
10' Clg.

Family Room
14'-8" x 19'-4"
14' Clg.

Desk

Kitchen
14' x 11'

Pantry

Dining
11' x 14'
11' Clg.

Desk

Util.

Bath 2

Linen

Living Room
15' x 19'-4"
11' Clg.

Foyer

Bedroom 3
11'-4" x 13'

Bedroom 2
12' x 11'
11' Clg.

Design Z9807
Square Footage: 2,785

● The balance and symmetry of this European home has an inviting quality about it. An entry foyer allowing a grand view out of the back of the house leads directly to the great room. Just off the great room are a convenient and functional gourmet kitchen and a bright, adjoining bay-windowed breakfast room. The master suite enjoys privacy in its position at the rear of the home. Three other bedrooms, one which might serve as a guest room or children's den and one that might work well as a study, round out the sleeping accommodations.

Design by
Design Traditions

Family Room Perspective

Design Z9800

First Floor: 1,231 square feet
Second Floor: 1,154 square feet
Total: 2,385 square feet

● All the Old World elements of gables, dormer windows, stone work, multi-level roof and spires combine to create this charming cottage. The main focal point of the foyer is the large formal dining room with its beautiful triple window combination. The family room features a beamed ceiling, fireplace, and convenient back staircase. The breakfast area has a bay window and a door to the back deck, ideal for outdoor entertaining. The master suite has extended space with its own bay sitting area, roomy bath with whirlpool tub, and spacious closet. Other bedrooms share a bath. There is also a bonus room over the garage.

Design by
Design Traditions

Design Z9871

First Floor: 2,208 square feet
Second Floor: 1,250 square feet
Total: 3,458 square feet

Design by
Design Traditions

● As quaint, yet majestic as a country manor on the Rhine, this European-styled stucco home enjoys the enchantment of arched windows and finials to underscore its charm. The two-story foyer leads through French doors to the study with its own hearth and English-coffered ceiling. Coupling with this cozy refuge is the master suite with tray ceiling and large accommodating bath and closet. The large, sunken family room is highlighted by a fireplace, bookcases, lots of glass and easy access to a back stair and large gourmet kitchen. Upstairs are two bedrooms which share a connecting bath. A third, more spacious bedroom gives guests the ultimate in convenience with a private bath and walk-in closet.

Design by
Design Traditions

Design Z9825

First Floor: 2,129 square feet
Second Floor: 895 square feet
Total: 3,024 square feet

● Imposing in the style of country estates in Europe, this stucco exterior home makes a grand statement of architectural excitement. The foyer offers all an impressive view of the dining room, family room and through to the back of the house—all from one breath-taking perspective. The master suite promises privacy and comfort with its lively sitting room, awash in bright sunlight from its many windows. French doors leading to the back deck complete this ideal private retreat. The kitchen, with its vaulted breakfast/sunroom area, allows easy maneuverability. All guests will enjoy maximum comfort with the downstairs guest room. Upstairs are two more bedrooms, plus storage space, and a large, sunny playroom overlooking the breakfast area below.

Design Z9275

First Floor: 1,602 square feet
Second Floor: 654 square feet
Total: 2,256 square feet

● From the beautiful bay window in the dining room to the French doors connecting the formal living room to the family room with fireplace, built-in bookshelves and entertainment center, this home delivers a wealth of amenities. An open dinette sits adjacent to the kitchen which features a snack bar and pantry. The master suite has a boxed ceiling and skylit master dressing/bath area with decorator plant ledge, double vanity and windowed whirlpool. The first-floor laundry is conveniently placed. Bedroom 2 upstairs echoes the bay window in the dining room. Three second-floor bedrooms share a compartmented bath with two lavatories.

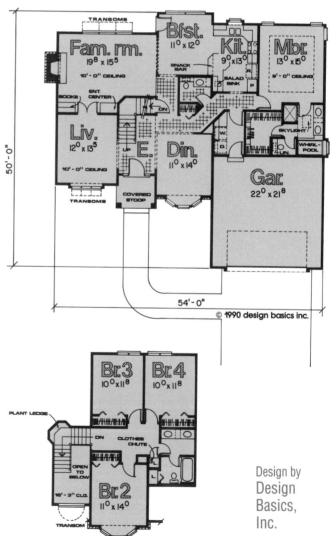

Design by
Design
Basics,
Inc.

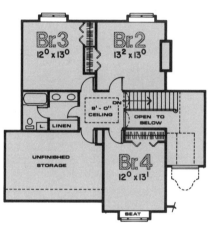

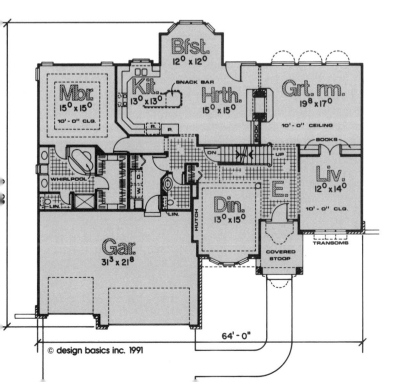

Design Z9326

First Floor: 2,073 square feet
Second Floor: 741 square feet
Total: 2,814 square feet

● Striking! From the curbside of this 1½-story home, brick and stucco accents command attention. Sunlight pours through the bayed window in the dining room with hutch space. Ten-foot ceilings enhance the elegant living room and comfortable great room which are separated via French doors. Practical! Family-oriented features in the great room include a through-fireplace and bookcases. Special features in the bayed breakfast/gourmet kitchen/hearth room combination include a snack bar, built-in bookshelves and generous counter space. The main floor master suite offers a tiered ceiling, huge walk-in closet and corner whirlpool, plus His and Hers vanities. Three generous secondary bedrooms share a compartmented bath.

Design by
Design
Basics,
Inc.

125

◄ 63' ►

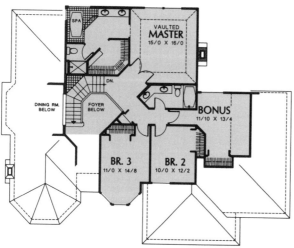

NOOK
11/0 X 14/0
9' CLG. TYP.

FAMILY
16/0 X 15/6

13/6 X 14/2

REF.
T.C.
PAN. DESK
WET BAR

50'

Vaulted
DINING
12/8 X 11/0

UP

LIN.

LIVING
13/4 X 17/9

DEN
11/0 X 14/6

GARAGE
30/4 X 22/8 +/-

Design by
Alan Mascord
Design Associates, Inc.

SPA

VAULTED
MASTER
15/0 X 16/0

DINING RM.
BELOW

FOYER
BELOW

DN.

BONUS
11/10 X 13/4

BR. 3
11/0 X 14/8

BR. 2
10/0 X 12/2

Design Z9478

First Floor: 1,586 square feet
Second Floor: 960 square feet
Total: 2,546 square feet
Bonus Room: 194 square feet

● This exquisite plan features two
tower structures that enhance its
dramatic facade. Inside, it contains
a beautifully functioning room
arrangement that caters to family
lifestyles. The living areas radiate
around the central hallway which
also contains the stairway to the
second floor. The areas are large,
open and convenient for both casual and formal occasions. Three bedrooms upstairs include two family
bedrooms and a grand master suite
with a bath fit for a king. An oversized walk-in closet and vaulted
ceiling are found here. Bonus space
over the garage can be developed
at a later time to suit changing
needs.

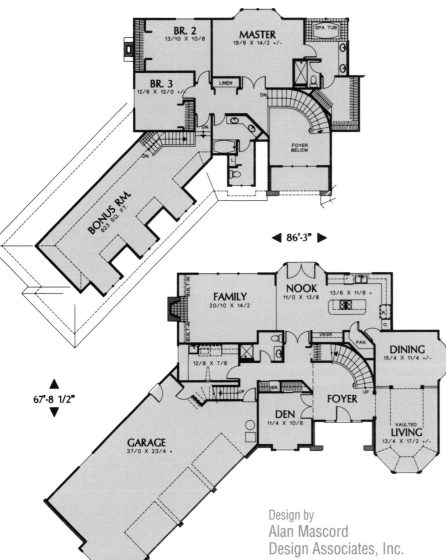

BR. 2
13/10 X 10/8

MASTER
19/6 X 14/2 +/-

SPA TUB

BR. 3
12/6 X 12/0 +/-

LINEN

DN.

DN.

DN.

DN.

FOYER
BELOW

BONUS RM.
623 SQ. FT.

◀ 86'-3" ▶

FAMILY
20/10 X 14/2

NOOK
11/0 X 13/8

13/6 X 11/8 +

BUILT-IN

BUILT-IN

DESK

PAN.

DINING
15/4 X 11/4 +/-

12/8 X 7/6

UP

BR.

UP

DEN
11/4 X 10/8

FOYER

67'-8 1/2"

▲
▼

GARAGE
37/0 X 23/4 +

VAULTED
LIVING
13/4 X 17/2 +/-

Design Z9440

First Floor: 1,758 square feet
Second Floor: 1,109 square feet
Total: 2,867 square feet
Bonus Room: 623 square feet

● Representing expansive elegance in a timeless design, this home offers as its focal point a graciously curved staircase in its two-story foyer. A second stairway leads to bonus space over the garage. Besides spacious living areas on the first floor, there is a powder room with shower which allows the den to serve as a guest room when needed. The family room features a fireplace and built-ins. To the rear of the second floor is the master suite containing a bay window overlooking the rear yard and a deluxe bath with spa tub. Two family bedrooms share a compartmented bath. An oversized three-car garage provides enough room for a workshop or additional storage space.

Design by
Alan Mascord
Design Associates, Inc.

◄ **68'** ►

DINING
11/0 X 13/6
9' CLG.

APPLIANCE
GARAGE

10' CLG.
NOOK
9/4 X 11/4

11/8 X 15/6

9' CLG.

FAMILY RM.
17/8 X 15/6 +/-
10' CLG.

51'
▲
▼

**VAULTED
LIVING**
13/4 X 18/6

DESK

WET BAR

BUILT-IN

W. D.

DEN
10/8 X 11/10
9' CLG.

GARAGE
26/0 X 28/6 +

UP

SPA

BR. 2
13/0 X 12/0
9' CLG.

LIN.

MASTER
17/8 X 15/6
10' CLG.

8' CLG.

LIN.

DN.

UP

LIN.

SKYLITE

BR. 3
10/8 X 13/0
9' CLG.

FOYER BELOW

**VAULTED
BONUS RM.**
21/0 X 13/0

Design Z9400

First Floor: 1,618 square feet
Second Floor: 1,212 square feet
Bonus Room: 376 square feet
Total: 3,206 square feet

● This attractive European-styled plan
has a stucco finish and arched windows
complementing the facade. Nine-foot
ceilings are standard throughout both
levels with some areas, such as the
nook, family room and master bedroom,
having ten-foot ceilings. From the two-
story foyer with its angled stair, look to
the dramatically vaulted living room on
one side and den with French doors on
the other. Upstairs a sumptuous master
suite includes spa tub, shower and large
walk-in closet. Over the garage is a
vaulted bonus room, perfect as a game
or hobby room.

Design by
Alan Mascord
Design Associates, Inc.

127

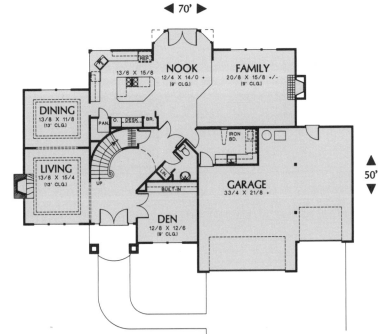

BR. 3
13/2 X 13/4
(9' CLG.)

BR. 2
12/4 X 12/6
(9' CLG.)

MASTER
17/2 X 15/8
(9' CLG.)

DN.

LINEN

SPA

FOYER
BELOW

BR. 4
12/8 X 11/0 +
(9' CLG.)

◀ 70' ▶

HP

NOOK
13/6 X 15/8

FAMILY
20/8 X 15/8 +/-
(9' CLG.)

DINING
13/8 X 11/8
(13' CLG.)

PAN. D. DESK BR.

IRON
BD.

LIVING
13/8 X 15/4
(13' CLG.)

UP

BUILT-IN

GARAGE
33/4 X 21/8 +

DEN
12/8 X 12/6
(9' CLG.)

▲
50'
▼

Design Z9513

First Floor: 1,764 square feet
Second Floor: 1,393 square feet
Total: 3,157 square feet

● A volume entry gives way to an elegant
curving stairway. The formal living and dining
rooms with 13-foot-high tray ceilings are to the
left, while a den with built-ins is to the right.
An angled powder room with linen storage is
placed conveniently near the foyer. Double
doors lead to the spacious kitchen, breakfast
nook and family room combination. Fireplaces
are located in both the living and family rooms.
The laundry room includes a sink and a built-
in ironing board. Four bedrooms occupy the
second floor, including a master bedroom with
9-foot tray ceiling. The master bath features a
spa tub, separate shower, dual vanities, walk-in
closet and a wide dressing area.

Design by
Alan Mascord
Design Associates, Inc.

130

Design Z8665
Square Footage: 2,799

● An impressive exterior leads to a grand interior. The living areas are highlighted by volume ceilings and double doors. A walk-in closet and nearby full bath add to the utility of the den. The central kitchen with island is convenient to the living, dining, breakfast and family rooms. The family room features a fireplace and access to the covered porch. Double doors lead to the segregated master bedroom with dual walk-in closets and a spacious bath with two vanities, whirlpool tub, separate shower and an attached solarium. Three family bedrooms and a full bath are to the right of the plan.

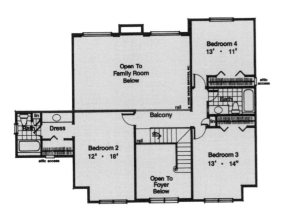

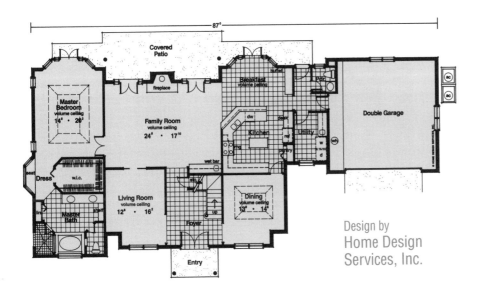

Design Z8654

First Floor: 2,212 square feet
Second Floor: 874 square feet
Total: 3,086 square feet

● From the moment you see this beautiful period home, you'll be reminded of the style and grace of the South. While keeping traditional design basics intact, the home is designed for today's lifestyles. The master suite is on the first floor and boasts a coffered-ceiling bed chamber. A bayed sitting area off the walk-in closet is perfect for morning coffee. The living and family areas are beautifully intermingled with double pocket doors into both spaces. The family room features French doors leading to the patio. Note the lavatory off the rear yard and the generous laundry room. Three bedrooms upstairs are perfect for family and guests.

Design by
Home Design
Services, Inc.

DECK

BREAKFAST
8'-4" X 10'-0"

KITCHEN
13'-4" X 16'-0"

GREAT ROOM
14'-6" X 19'-0"

MASTER BEDROOM
13'-4" X 17'-10"

LAUNDRY
8'-0" X 9'-0"

W.I.C.

MASTER BATH
10'-8" X 16'-4"

TWO CAR GARAGE
21'-4" X 21'-6"

DINING ROOM
12'-0" X 16'-0"

FOYER
7'-6" X 13'-6"

STUDY
11'-4" X 15'-2"

W.I.C.

BEDROOM NO. 4
13'-4" X 11'-6"

OPEN TO BELOW

BEDROOM NO. 3
15'-0" X 12'-0"

BATH

BEDROOM NO. 2
12'-4" X 13'-6"

OPEN TO BELOW

Copyright 1990 Stephen S. Fuller, Inc.

WIDTH 63'
DEPTH 51'

Design by
Design Traditions

Design Z9816

First Floor: 1,900 square feet
Second Floor: 800 square feet
Total: 2,700 square feet

● Through the blending of stucco and stacked stone, this Country French home represents a specific architectural motif with the repeated arch pattern evident in the windows and doorway transom. The foyer is flanked by the spacious dining room and study which is accented by a warming fireplace and vaulted ceiling. A great room with a full wall of glass brings the outdoors inside. Adjacent to the great room is the breakfast area; its generous use of windows and volume ceiling make it feel more like a sunroom extension for the spacious kitchen. The master suite of this home is strategically located on the main level providing the ultimate in convenience and privacy. A large accommodating bath offers separate vanities and individual closet areas. The upstairs of this livable plan has three bedrooms, large walk-in closets and a shared bath which allows for maximum privacy.

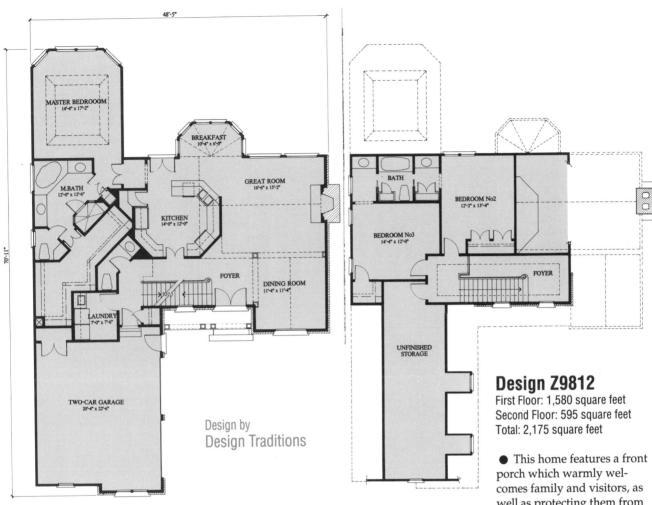

MASTER BEDROOOM
14'-4" x 17'-2"

BREAKFAST
10'-4" x 6'-0"

GREAT ROOM
16'-6" x 15'-2"

M.BATH
12'-0" x 12'-6"

KITCHEN
14'-0" x 12'-0"

FOYER

DINING ROOM
11'-4" x 11'-4"

LAUNDRY
7'-0" x 7'-6"

TWO-CAR GARAGE
20'-4" x 22'-6"

48'-5"

70'-11"

Design by
Design Traditions

BATH

BEDROOM No2
12'-2" x 13'-4"

BEDROOM No3
14'-4" x 12'-6"

FOYER

UNFINISHED
STORAGE

Design Z9812

First Floor: 1,580 square feet
Second Floor: 595 square feet
Total: 2,175 square feet

● This home features a front porch which warmly welcomes family and visitors, as well as protecting them from the weather—a true Southern Original. Inside, the spacious foyer leads directly to a large vaulted great room with massive fireplace. The dining room also receives the vaulted ceiling treatment. The grand kitchen offers both storage and large work areas opening up to the breakfast room. In the privacy and quiet of the rear of the home is the master suite with its garden bath, His and Hers vanities and oversized closet. The second floor provides two additional bedrooms with a shared bath along with a balcony overlook to the foyer below.

Design Z9834

First Floor: 1,355 square feet
Second Floor: 1,360 square feet
Total: 2,715 square feet

● The appeal of this home is definitely European and its interior is open and inviting. The formal living room and dining room are separated only by decorative columns. To the left of the foyer is the comfortable family room with a large fireplace and open rail detailing allowing access to the breakfast room and kitchen. An open staircase to the gallery above leads to a grand master suite with tray ceiling and luxurious bath with whirlpool tub, His and Hers vanities and a large walk-in closet. Two bedrooms with a connecting bath and a third bedroom with a private bath complete the room arrangements.

WIDTH 52'
DEPTH 49'

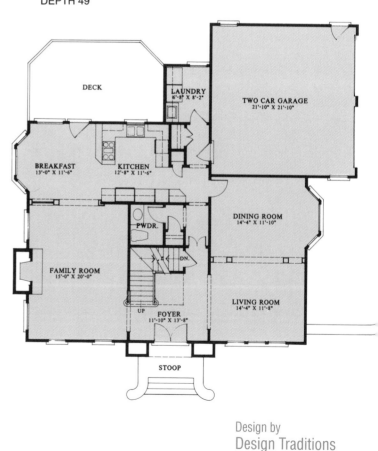

Design by
Design Traditions

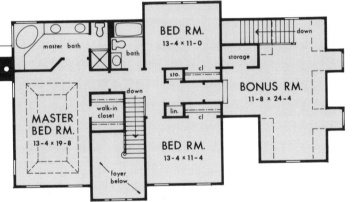

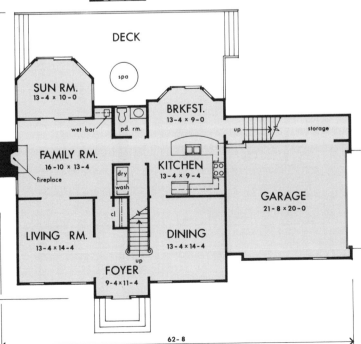

Design Z9653

First Floor: 1,355 square feet
Second Floor: 1,001 square feet
Total: 2,356 square feet
Bonus Room: 400 square feet

● The elegance of this traditional home is enhanced by the large double-hung windows and stucco veneer. The formal spaces such as the living room and dining room are directly accessible from the two-level entrance foyer. The more informal spaces can access the second level by means of a back stairway located in the rear of the house for privacy. The kitchen layout is U-shaped for maximum efficiency. The family room has a wet bar and a fireplace along with direct access to the sun room. A luxurious master bedroom features a tray ceiling and a large walk-in closet. Two other bedrooms share a full bath.

Design by
Donald A.
Gardner,
Architect, Inc.

Design Z9398

First Floor: 1,369 square feet
Second Floor: 1,711 square feet
Total: 3,080 square feet

● A bright, volume entry is
flanked by formal rooms, each with
special windows. A curved landing
on the staircase overlooks the family room. French doors link the living room and family room with
bayed window, fireplace and built-
in bookshelves. A bayed breakfast
area is adjacent to the kitchen with
dual pantries, desk and island
snack bar. The laundry room
comes complete with a sink and an
iron-a-way. The second floor provides five bedrooms, including a
deluxe master suite with French
doors into a sitting room or nursery. Two compartmented
Hollywood baths serve the four
family bedrooms, while the master
bath features an oval whirlpool
under an arched window, His and
Hers vanities and decorator plant
ledges.

Design by
Design
Basics,
Inc.

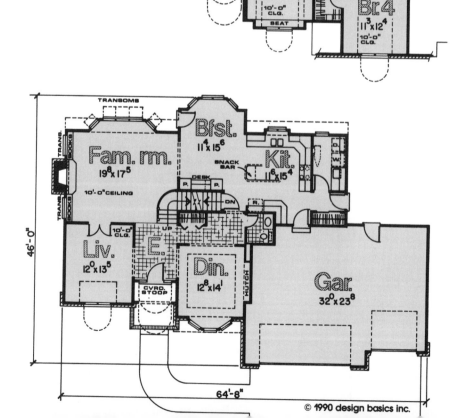

© 1990 design basics inc.

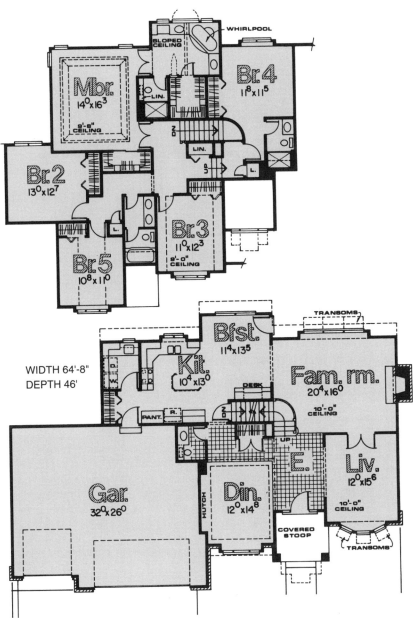

WIDTH 64'-8"
DEPTH 46'

Design Z9383

First Floor: 1,335 square feet
Second Floor: 1,475 square feet
Total: 2,810 square feet

● This dynamic elevation has instant curb appeal. The entry is flanked by the formal living room and the formal dining room with hutch space. French doors between the living room and family room add charm. A warming fireplace and sparkling picture/awning windows with transoms above highlight the family room. The island kitchen features a Lazy Susan, planning desk, pantry and an adjacent breakfast room. The window-lit laundry includes a sink. A luxurious master suite, with a vaulted ceiling and two walk-in closets, includes a bath with whirlpool tub and His and Hers vanities. Four secondary bedrooms are found on the second floor. Bedroom 4 is up a few steps and features a private bath.

Design by
Design
Basics,
Inc.

Design Z3574

First Floor: 1,488 square feet
Second Floor: 1,590 square feet
Total: 3,078 square feet
Bonus Room: 264 square feet

Design by
Home Planners,
Inc.

● An elongated entrance court complements the graceful exterior of this home. The two-story foyer introduces a magnificent open space made up of a gathering room—with a fireplace—and a dining room. Both areas access the terrace. For family pursuits, a rear family room provides a pleasant hearth and passage to the porch. Nearby, the U-shaped island kitchen enjoys a breakfast room and a

nearby laundry room. On the second floor, four bedrooms accommodate family and guests alike. The master suite utilizes a private bath with a whirlpool tub while another bedroom also features its own bath. Also notable about this design is the bonus room which may be built in place of the one-car garage.

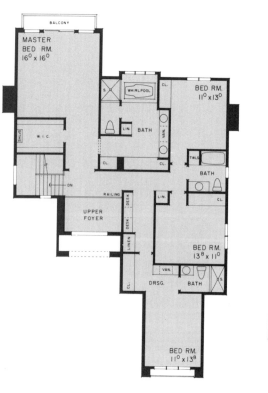

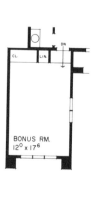

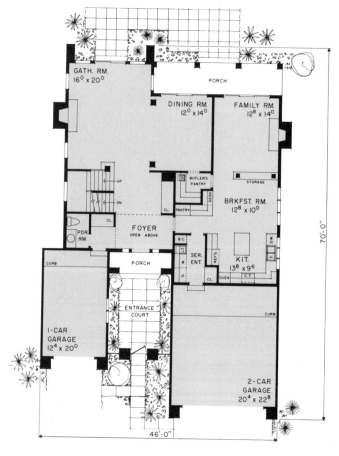

Design Z3573

First Floor: 1,650 square feet
Second Floor: 1,508 square feet
Total: 3,158 square feet
Bonus Room: 275 square feet
Bedroom: 176 square feet

Design by
Home Planners,
Inc.

● A design for the times, this beautiful transitional home may be built with a fourth bedroom and/or a first-floor bonus room. The entrance court introduces a covered porch. Inside, the tiled foyer offers a dramatic space comprised of a dining room on the left and, separated by a staircase, a living room on the right. Both rooms enjoy their own terrace. Casual living takes off in the family room with its terrace. An expansive kitchen backs up the plan and includes a walk-in pantry and an island countertop. Upstairs, overlooking the dining room, a hallway branches off into three bedrooms, including a delightful master suite. Here, highlights range from two balconies to a bath with a whirlpool tub.

ENTRANCE COURT

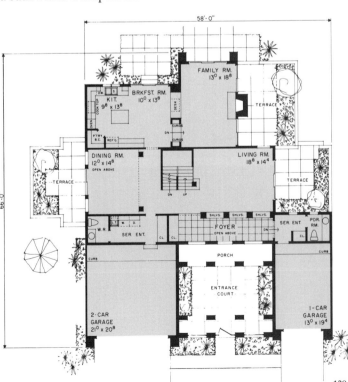

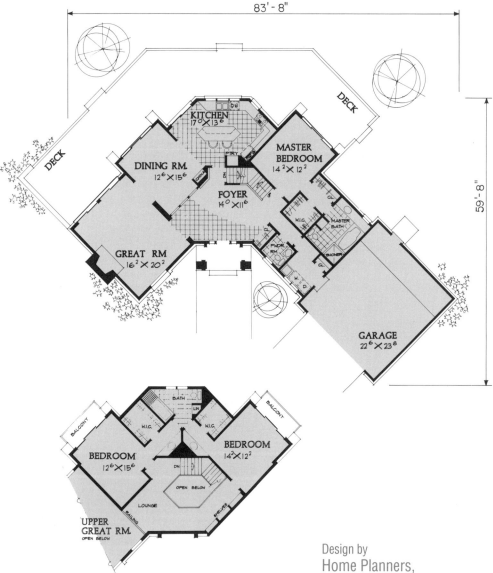

83' - 8"

59' - 8"

DECK

DECK

DECK

KITCHEN
17⁰ X 13⁶

DINING RM.
12⁶ X 15⁶

MASTER
BEDROOM
14² X 12²

FOYER
14⁰ X 11⁶

GREAT RM.
16² X 20²

W.I.C.

MASTER
BATH

PWDR.
RM.

SHOWER

GARAGE
22⁶ X 23⁸

BATH

BALCONY

W.I.C.

W.I.C.

BALCONY

BEDROOM
12⁶ X 15⁶

BEDROOM
14² X 12²

DN

OPEN BELOW

LOUNGE

RAILING

SHELVES

UPPER
GREAT RM.
OPEN BELOW

Design Z3310

First Floor: 1,668 square feet
Second Floor: 905 square feet
Total: 2,573 square feet

● If you're looking for a different angle on a new home, try this enchanting transitional house. The open foyer creates a rich atmosphere. To the left you'll find a great room with raised brick hearth and sliding glass doors that lead out onto a wraparound deck. The kitchen heads up the first floor and includes a snack bar and deck access. The master bedroom, with balcony and bath with whirlpool, is located on the first floor for privacy. Upstairs, two family bedrooms, both with balconies and walk-in closets, share a full bath. Don't overlook the lounge and elliptical window that give the second floor added charisma.

Design by
Home Planners,
Inc.

Tudor Home Plans

Tudor style draws upon a number of Medieval English models, ranging from small country cottages to expansive manor houses. This popular style was first adopted by wealthy Americans in the late 1880s. The development of masonry veneering after World War I enabled modest suburban homes to sport Tudor characteristics.

One of the most easily identifiable house styles, Tudor has two true marks of distinction: a large, prominent and elaborate chimney and decorative half-timbering. Other Tudor characteristics include a side-gabled roof, prominent cross gable, casement windows with diamond-shaped panes and combinations of wall materials such as stucco, stone and brick.

A semi-circular doorway was so common on early Tudor houses that it came to be known as the "Tudor arch." Arched doorways with stone work still appear on contemporary Tudors. Tall windows in groups of three and bay windows often grace the front facade. The Elizabethan style, which is slightly less formal, features a half-timbered, overhanging second floor.

The beginning of this section presents several one-story Tudor homes, while the rest, like most Tudor designs, consist of two-stories. The designs in this section range in size from 2,211 to 3,355 square feet.

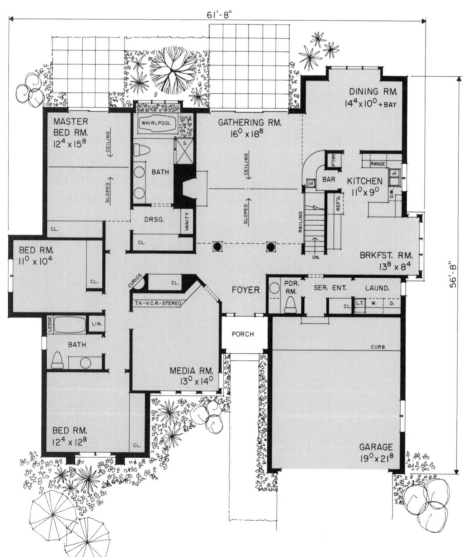

Design Z3377
Square Footage: 2,217

● This Tudor design provides a handsome exterior comple- mented by a spacious and mod- ern floor plan. The sleeping area is positioned to the left side of the home. The master bedroom features an elegant bath with whirlpool, shower, dual lavs and a separate vanity area. Two family bedrooms share a full bath. A media room exhibits the TV, VCR and stereo. The enormous gathering room is set off by columns and contains a fireplace and sliding doors to the rear terrace. The dining room and breakfast room each feature a bay window.

Design by
Home Planners,
Inc.

Design Z2854

First Floor: 1,261 square feet
Second Floor: 950 square feet
Total: 2,211 square feet

Design by
Home Planners,
Inc.

● A fine sight, indeed. This is a story and a half, but the second floor has so much livability, it's more like a two-story plan. In addition to a large master suite, two kids' rooms and a second full bath, the second floor has a cozy spot that could serve as a lounge, nursery or play area. The first floor is solidly utilitarian: living room with fireplace, large separate dining room, family room, efficient U-shaped kitchen, study with nifty bay window and covered porch. For information on customizing this design, call 1-800-322-6797, ext. 800.

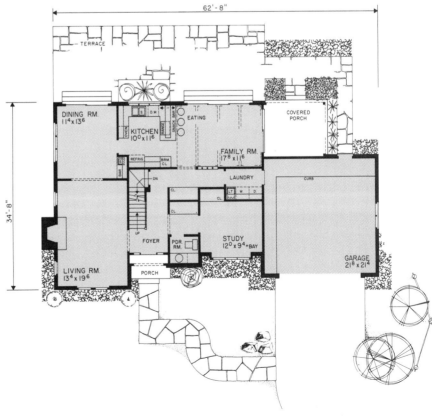

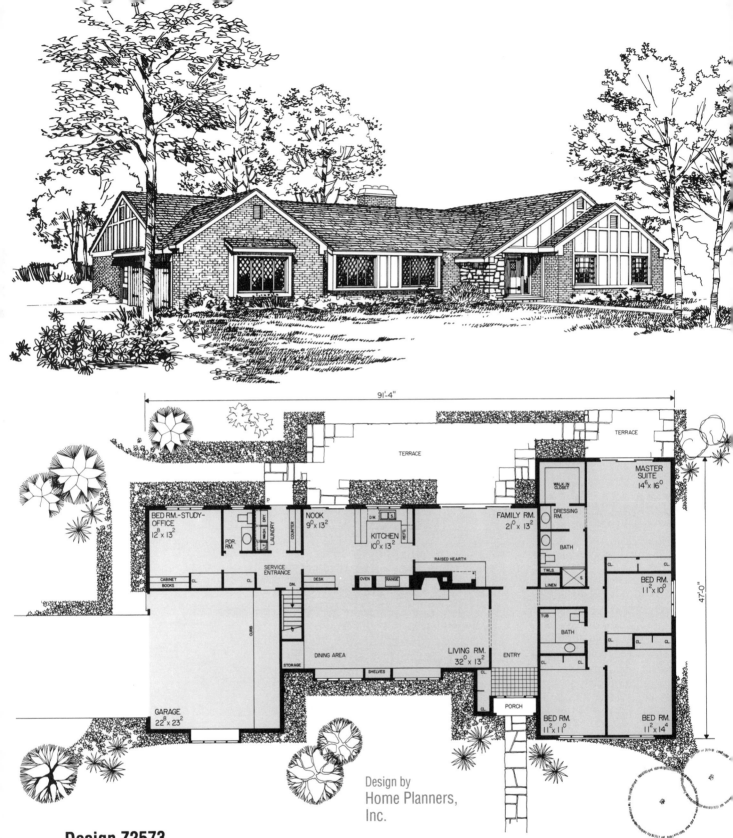

Design Z2573
Square Footage: 2,747

● A Tudor ranch! Combining brick and wood for an elegant look. It has a living/dining room measuring 32' by 13', large indeed. It is fully appointed with a traditional fireplace and built-in shelves, flanked by diagonally paned windows. There's much more! There is a family room with a raised hearth fireplace and sliding glass doors that open onto the terrace. A U-shaped kitchen has lots of built-ins . . . a range, an oven, a desk. Plus a separate breakfast nook. The sleeping facilities consist of three family bedrooms plus an elegant master bedroom suite. A conveniently located laundry with a folding counter is in the service entrance. Adjacent to the laundry is a washroom. The corner of the plan has a study or make it a fifth bedroom if you prefer.

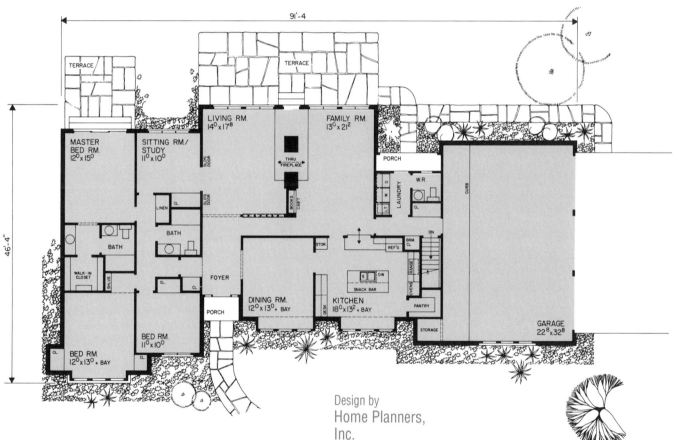

Design by
Home Planners,
Inc.

Design Z2785

Square Footage: 2,375

● Exceptional Tudor design! Passers-by will take a second glance at this fine home wherever it may be located. And the interior is just as pleasing. As one enters the foyer and looks around, the plan will speak for itself in the areas of convenience and efficiency.

Cross room traffic will be avoided. There is a hall leading to each of the three bedrooms and study of the sleeping wing and another leading to the living room, family room, kitchen and laundry with washroom. The formal dining room can be entered from both

the foyer and the kitchen. Efficiency will be the by-word when describing the kitchen. Note the fine features: a built-in desk, pantry, island snack bar with sink and pass-thru to the family room. The fireplace will be enjoyed in the living and family rooms.

Design Z9820

First Floor: 1,410 square feet
Second Floor: 1,490 square feet
Total: 2,900 square feet

● To highlight the exterior of this brick and stucco home, window jack arches have been combined with half-timbering to create a Royal English Estate. The main level of the home opens with a grand two-story foyer and formal living and dining areas located on the right. The living room and dining room are separated only by an arched open-

SITTING ROOM
12'-6" x 7'-8"

M.BATH
13'-0" x 13'-0"

MASTER BEDROOM
15'-10" x 13'-0"

BEDROOM No.3
12'-6" x 13'-0"

BATH

M.CLOSET

FOYER BELOW

BEDROOM No.4
11'-7" x 12'-1"

BEDROOM No.2
11'-4" x 12'-2"

BATH

DECK

WIDTH 57'-10"
DEPTH 42'-10"

BREAKFAST
12'-6" x 7'-8"

LAUNDRY
6'-6" x 10'-6"

KITCHEN
13'-0" x 10'-6"

TWO-CAR GARAGE
20'-4" x 21'-4"

FAMILY ROOM
15'-6" x 17'-4"

POWDER
5'-4" x 6'-8"

FOYER
14'-8" x 10'-10"

LIVING ROOM
11'-4" x 13'-8"

DINING ROOM
15'-11" x 12'-8"

STOOP

ing allowing for flow during entertaining. Conveniently, the more casual family room is located in the rear of the home and features a wet bar, fireplace and easy access to both the breakfast room and kitchen with ample cabinet space and light. The combination front and rear stairs from the main level lead to the master suite which has its own private sitting area and unusual volume ceiling. Two other bedrooms share a bath and feature individual vanity areas. The fourth bedroom includes its own bath making it an excellent guest suite with access right off the second-level foyer.

Design by
Design Traditions

WIDTH 50'
DEPTH 50'-6"

Design Z9819

First Floor: 1,678 square feet
Second Floor: 1,677 square feet
Total: 3,355 square feet

● This English Manor home features a dramatic brick and stucco exterior accented by gabled roofline and artful half-timbering. Inside, the foyer opens to the formal living room accented with a

Design by
Design Traditions

vaulted ceiling and boxed bay window. The dining room flows directly off the living room and features its own angled bay window. Through the double doors lies the center of family activity. An entire wall of glass, accented by a central fireplace, spans from the family room through to the breakfast area and kitchen. For your guests, a bedroom and bath are located on the main level. The second floor provides two additional bedrooms and a bath for children. The master suite with a tray ceiling, fireplace and private study is a retreat. The master bath has separate vanities, garden tub and separate shower along with oversized His and Hers closets.

Design Z3335

First Floor: 1,504 square feet
Second Floor: 1,348 square feet
Total: 2,852 square feet

● This is a first-rate Tudor with three bedrooms upstairs and casual and formal living downstairs. Corner fireplaces in the family room and living room will be favorite gathering spots. From the efficient U-shaped kitchen move to a convenient service area and two-car garage.

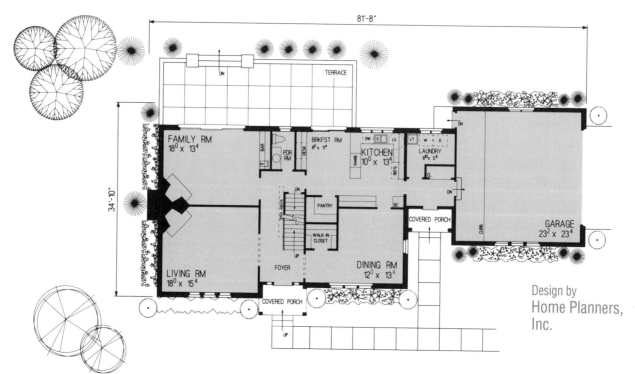

Design by
Home Planners,
Inc.

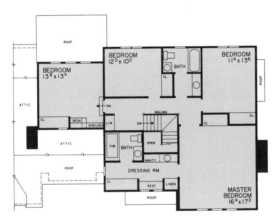

Design by
Home Planners,
Inc.

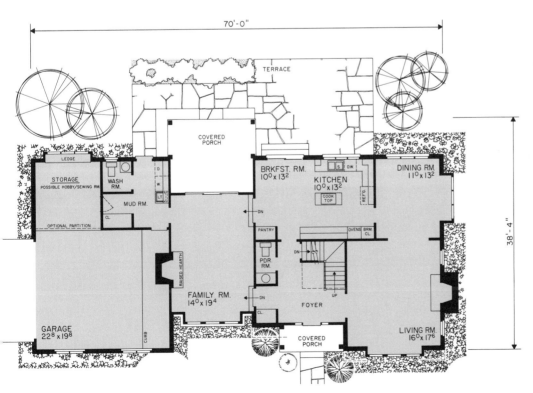

Design Z2855

First Floor: 1,372 square feet
Second Floor: 1,245 square feet
Total: 2,617 square feet

● This elegant Tudor
house is perfect for the
family who wants to move-
up in living area, style and
luxury. As you enter this
home you will find a large
living room with a fire-
place on your right. Adjacent, the formal dining
room has easy access to
both the living room and
the kitchen. The kitchen/
breakfast room has an open
plan and access to the rear
terrace. Sunken a few
steps, the spacious family
room is highlighted with a
fireplace and access to the
rear, covered porch. Note
the optional planning of
the garage storage area.
Plan this area according to
the needs of your family.
Upstairs, your family will
enjoy three bedrooms and
a full bath, along with a
spacious master bedroom
suite. Truly a house that
will bring many years of
pleasure to your family.
For information on customizing this design, call 1-800-
322-6797, ext. 800.

● This is an exquisitely styled Tudor tri-level designed to serve its happy occupants for many years. The contrasting use of material surely makes the exterior eye-catching.

Design Z2847 Main Level: 1,874 square feet
Lower Level: 1,131 square feet; Total: 3,005 square feet

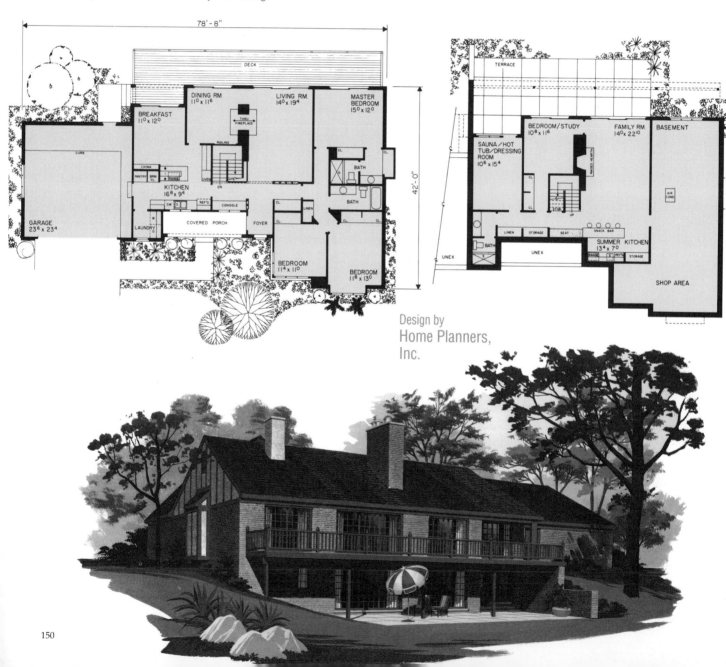

Design by
Home Planners,
Inc.

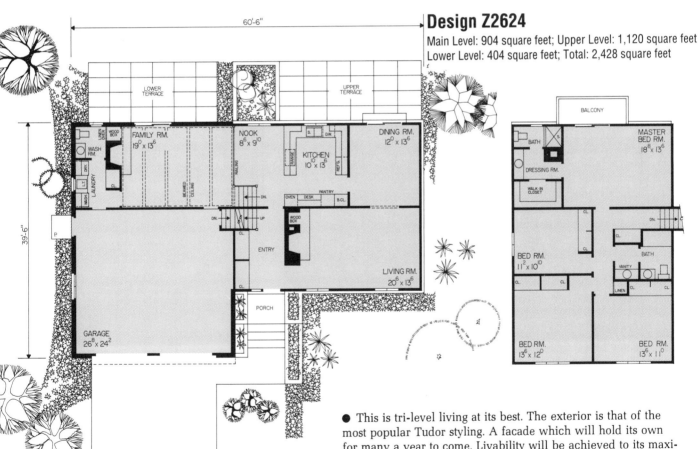

Design Z2624

Main Level: 904 square feet; Upper Level: 1,120 square feet
Lower Level: 404 square feet; Total: 2,428 square feet

Design by
Home Planners,
Inc.

● This is tri-level living at its best. The exterior is that of the most popular Tudor styling. A facade which will hold its own for many a year to come. Livability will be achieved to its maximum on the four (including basement) levels. The occupants of the master bedroom can enjoy the outdoors on their private balcony. Additional outdoor enjoyment can be gained on the two terraces. That family room is more than 19' x 13' and includes a beamed ceiling and fireplace with wood box. Its formal companion, the living room, is similar in size and also will have the added warmth of a fireplace.

Design Z9372

First Floor: 1,933 square feet
Second Floor: 646 square feet
Total: 2,579 square feet

● Stone and stucco coupled with excellent lines add intriguing curb appeal to the exterior of this home. The hall entry surveys the formal dining room, with built-in hutch space, and the great room with its through-fireplace, built-in entertainment center, and wet bar/servery. The kitchen is open to a hearth room and breakfast room with tiered ceiling. A convenient utility area leads to the three-car garage. The master bedroom, on the main floor, shares a hall containing built-in bookcases with the den. The master bath includes a whirlpool tub, separate shower, dual vanities and a walk-in closet. Three secondary bedrooms feature large closets and share a compartmented bath with dual lavatories.

Design by
Design
Basics,
Inc.

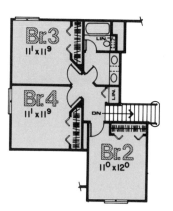

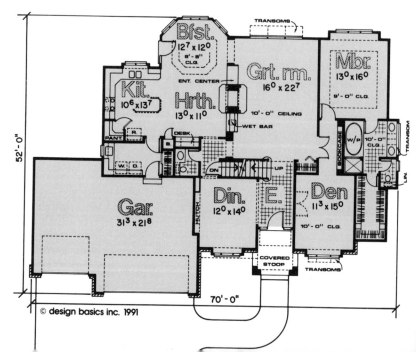

Spanish & Mediterranean Designs

Popular in parts of California, Florida and the Southwest, Spanish-style houses have an informal, easy-to-like ambience. Spanish and Mediterranean designs share certain architectural details, whether they be Spanish Mission, Monterey, Territorial, Santa Fe or Pueblo-style homes.

Architectural themes for various types of Spanish designs are borrowed from early mission churches. Mission-style homes have a distinctive red or orange tile roof created with half-cylinder tiles placed with every other one curved-side down. Other red tile roofs are made from Spanish tiles, which are S-shaped.

While there are many variations of Spanish and Mediterranean designs, common characteristics include an asymmetrical facade of stucco or adobe mud over a wood frame, a low-pitched roof, arches, wrought iron and heavy, wood-paneled doors.

One of the key features of Spanish designs is outdoor living space. Patios, interior courtyards, exterior porches and balconies, gardens, fountains and terraces are some of the many ways to bring the outdoors in.

The updated Spanish and Mediterranean designs in this section continue to provide indoor/outdoor livability, with special consideration toward easy access for those who wish to build a swimming pool in the rear yard. Design Z2670 on page 158 includes an interior atrium that pleases plant lovers and brings light to several living areas in the home.

Design Z8653

Square Footage: 2,962

● Enter the formal foyer of this home and you are greeted with a traditional split living room/dining room layout. But the family room is where the real living takes place. It explodes onto the outdoor living space which features a summer kitchen. The ultimate master suite contains coffered ceilings, a "boomerang" vanity and angular mirrors that reflect the bayed soaking tub and shower. Efficient use of space creates a huge closet with little dead center space. The three-bedroom family wing contains one bedroom with a private bath for the ultimate privacy for guests. Two other bedrooms share a lavish bath that accesses the rear patio.

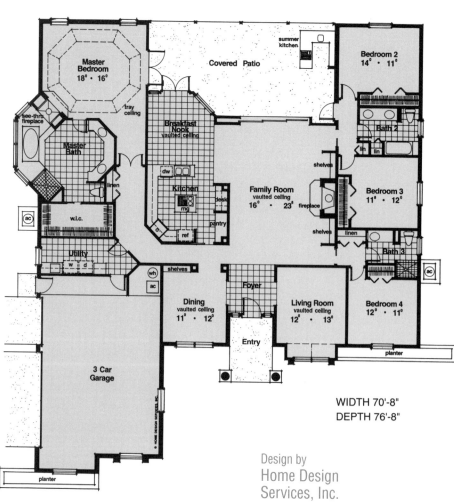

WIDTH 70'-8"
DEPTH 76'-8"

Design by
Home Design
Services, Inc.

Design Z8645

Square Footage: 2,224

● Arches crowned by gentle, hipped rooflines provide an Italianate charm in this bright, spacious, family-oriented plan. A covered entry leads to the foyer that presents the angular, vaulted living and dining rooms. A wet bar in the living room enhances livability. A kitchen with V-shape counter includes a walk-in pantry and looks out over the breakfast nook and family room with a fireplace. The master suite features a sitting area, two walk-in closets and a full bath with garden tub. Two additional bedrooms share a full bath located between them. A fourth bedroom, with its own bath, opens off the family room and works perfectly as a guest room.

Design Z8642
Square Footage: 2,734

● This home has an award-winning, sophisticated design. From the moment you enter, you know you are in a well-designed home. Besides a formal living area with covered patio nearby and formal dining area to the front, there is a family room with corner fireplace. It attaches directly to the breakfast room and kitchen. The bedrooms are split with family bedrooms to the right of the plan and the master suite to the left. The master bath has an angled entry, walk-in closet and spa tub. Blueprints for this home come with two different elevations and a large and small floor plan.

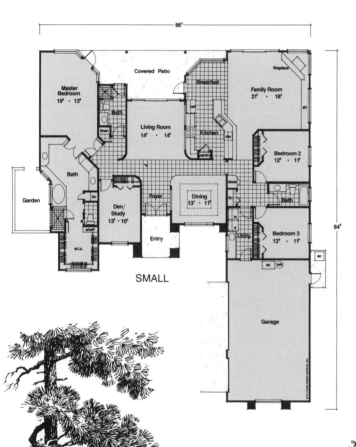

SMALL

LARGE

Design by
Home Design
Services, Inc.

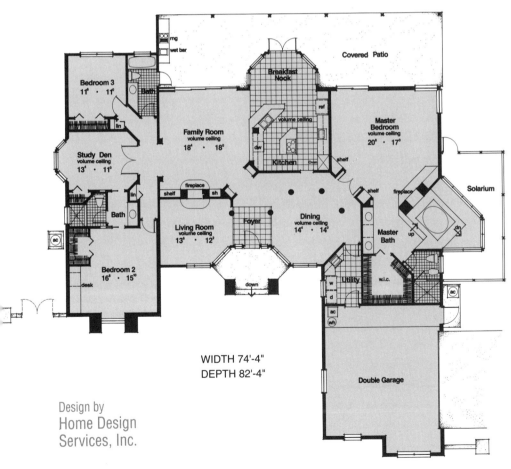

WIDTH 74'-4"
DEPTH 82'-4"

Design by
Home Design
Services, Inc.

Bedroom 3
11⁴ · 11⁴

Study Den
volume ceiling
13⁴ · 11⁰

Bath

Bedroom 2
16⁴ · 15¹⁰

desk

Family Room
volume ceiling
18⁴ · 18⁰

fireplace

shelf   sh

Living Room
volume ceiling
13⁴ · 12²

Foyer

down

Breakfast
Nook

volume ceiling

Kitchen

dw

ref

Dining
volume ceiling
14⁴ · 14⁰

shelf

Master
Bedroom
volume ceiling
20⁴ · 17⁰

shelf   fireplace

Solarium

up   dn

Master
Bath

w.i.c.

Utility

w
d

ac
wh

Double Garage

Covered Patio

mg

wet bar

Design Z8624
Square Footage: 2,987

● Classic columns, a tiled roof and beautiful arched windows herald a gracious interior for this fine home. Arched windows mark the entrance into the vaulted living room with a tiled fireplace. The dining room opens off the foyer with vaulted ceiling and lovely arched windows. The family room abounds with light from a wall of sliding glass doors that leads to the covered patio (note the wet bar and range that enhance outdoor living). The kitchen features a vaulted ceiling and unfolds into the roomy nook which boasts French doors onto the patio. The master bedroom also has patio access and shares a dual fireplace with the master bath. A solarium lights this space. A vaulted study/bedroom sits between two additional bedrooms—all share a full bath.

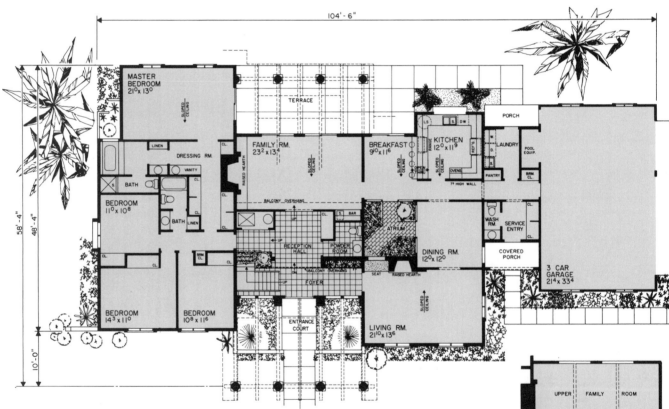

Design Z2670
Square Footage: 3,058

● A centrally located interior atrium is one of the most interesting features of this Spanish design. The atrium has a built-in seat and will bring light to its adjacent rooms; living, dining and breakfast. Beyond the foyer, sunken one step, is a tiled reception hall that includes a powder room. This area leads to the sleeping wing and up one step to the family room. Overlooking the family room is a railed lounge, 279 square feet, which can be used for various activities. The work center area will be convenient to work in.

Design Z2820

Square Footage: 2,261

● A privacy wall around the courtyard with pool and trellised planter area is a gracious area by which to enter this one-story design. The Spanish flavor is accented by the grillework and the tiled roof. Interior livability has a great deal to offer. The front living room has slid-ing glass doors which open to the en-trance court; the adjacent dining room features a bay window. Informal activ-ities will be enjoyed in the rear family room. Its many features include a slop-ed, beamed ceiling, raised hearth fire-place, sliding glass doors to the terrace and a snack bar for those very infor-mal meals. A laundry and powder room are adjacent to the U-shaped kitchen. The sleeping wing can remain quiet away from the plan's activity centers. Notice the three-car garage with an extra storage area.

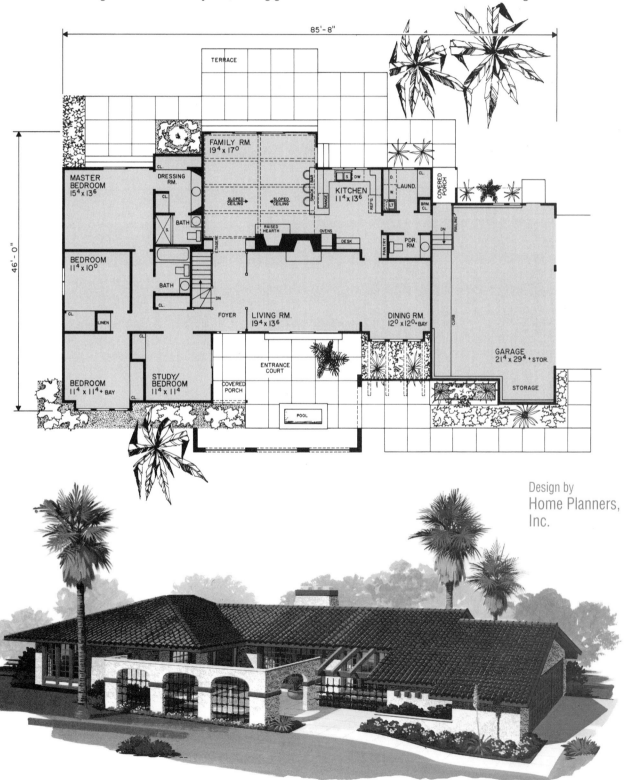

Design by
Home Planners,
Inc.

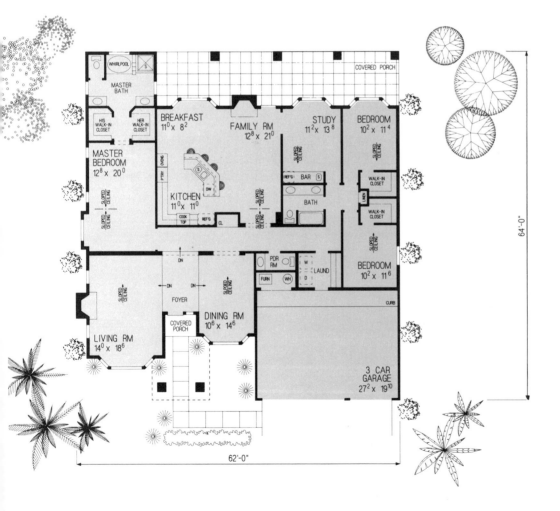

Design Z3413
Square Footage: 2,517

● Though distinctly Southwest in design, this home has some features that are universally appealing. Note, for instance, the central gallery, perpendicular to the raised entry hall, and running almost the entire width of the house. An L-shaped, angled kitchen serves the breakfast room and family room in equal fashion. Sleeping areas are found in four bedrooms including an optional study and exquisite master suite. For information on customizing this design, call 1-800-322-6797, ext. 800.

Design by
Home Planners,
Inc.

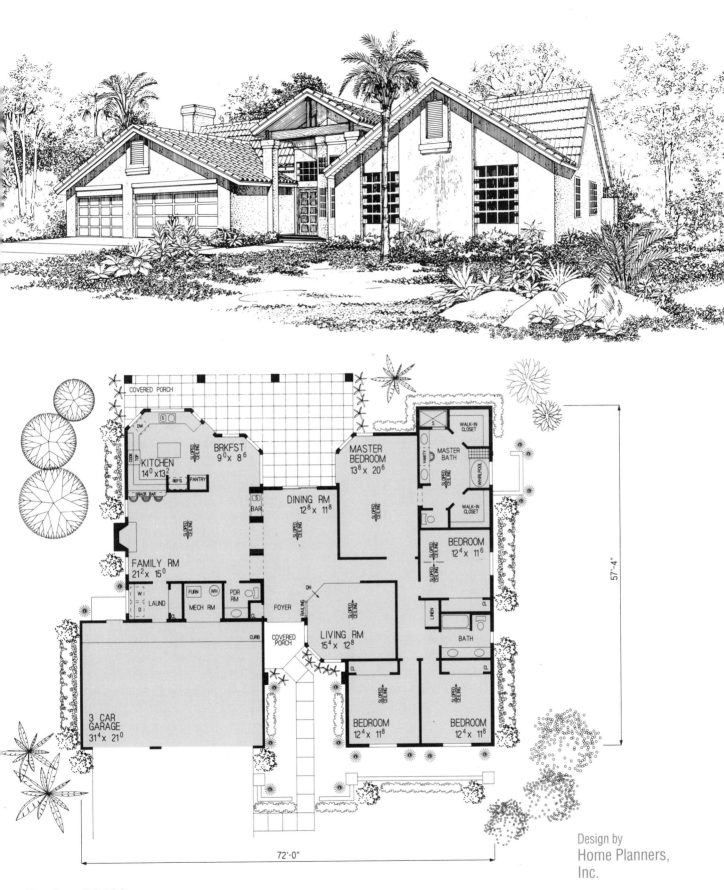

Design Z3423 Square Footage: 2,577

● This spacious Southwestern home will be a pleasure to come home to. Immediately off the foyer are the dining room and step-down living room with bay window. The highlight of the four-bedroom sleeping area is the master suite with porch access and a whirlpool for soaking away the day's worries. The informal living area features an enormous family room with fireplace and bay-windowed kitchen and breakfast room. Notice the snack bar pass-through to the family room. For information on customizing this design, call 1-800-322-6797, ext. 800.

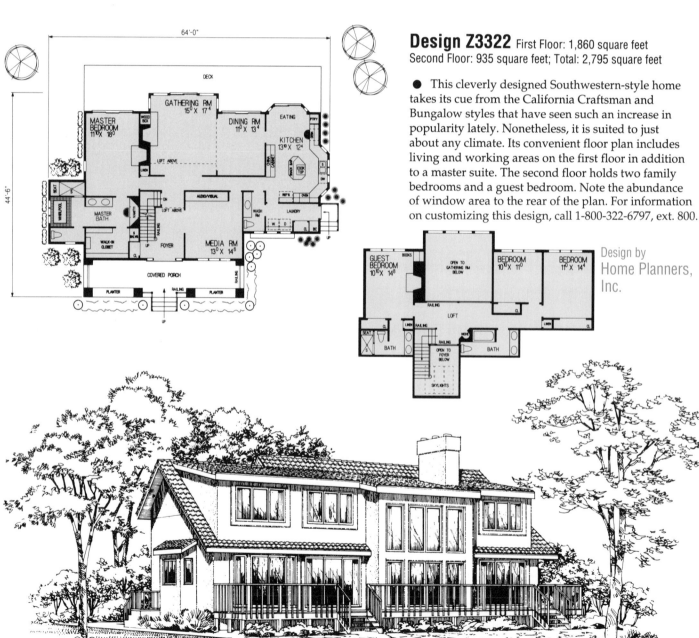

Design Z3322 First Floor: 1,860 square feet
Second Floor: 935 square feet; Total: 2,795 square feet

● This cleverly designed Southwestern-style home takes its cue from the California Craftsman and Bungalow styles that have seen such an increase in popularity lately. Nonetheless, it is suited to just about any climate. Its convenient floor plan includes living and working areas on the first floor in addition to a master suite. The second floor holds two family bedrooms and a guest bedroom. Note the abundance of window area to the rear of the plan. For information on customizing this design, call 1-800-322-6797, ext. 800.

Design by
Home Planners, Inc.

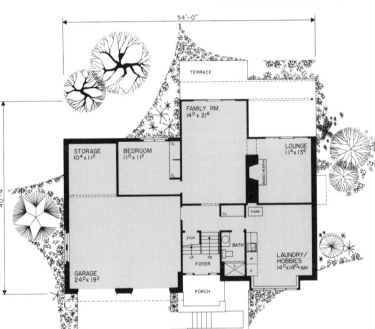

Design Z2843

Upper Level: 1,861 square feet
Lower Level: 1,181 square feet
Total: 3,042 square feet

● Bi-level living will be enjoyed to its fullest in this Spanish styled design. There is a lot of room for the various family activities. Informal living will take place on the lower level in the family room and lounge. The formal living and dining rooms, sharing a thru-fire-place, are located on the upper level.

Design by
Home Planners,
Inc.

Design Z3463

First Floor: 1,163 square feet
Second Floor: 1,077 square feet
Total: 2,240 square feet

● A clerestory round-top window brightens the foyer of this home. The living areas are well-planned and flow together. The two-story living room and the dining room with built-in curio cabinet are separated by elegant columns. The distinctive octagonal kitchen features an island with a snack bar, a pantry and easy access to the dining and breakfast rooms. The family room contains a fireplace and access to a covered rear porch. The master bedroom features a cozy fireplace, a deck and an amenity-filled bath with dual vanities, whirlpool tub, separate shower and a walk-in closet. Completing the second floor are two family bedrooms, a full bath and two built-in desks.

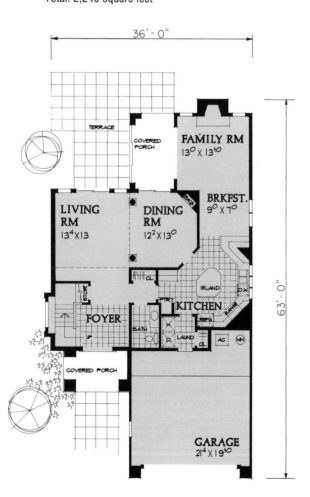

Design by
Home Planners,
Inc.

Design Z3464

First Floor: 1,776 square feet
Second Floor: 876 square feet
Total: 2,652 square feet

● If you're looking for something a little different from the rest, this dramatic home may end your search. A two-story foyer introduces an open formal area consisting of a volume living room and a dining room separated by columns. The kitchen sits to the rear of the plan and shares space with the breakfast room. Here, a curved wall adds interest—sliding glass doors take you out to a covered porch and a connecting terrace. The family room enjoys access to this terrace while maintaining great indoor livability with its see-through fireplace and volume ceiling. Also on the first floor, the master bedroom offers to its lucky occupants a pampering bath. The sleeping accommodations are complete with three upstairs bedrooms.

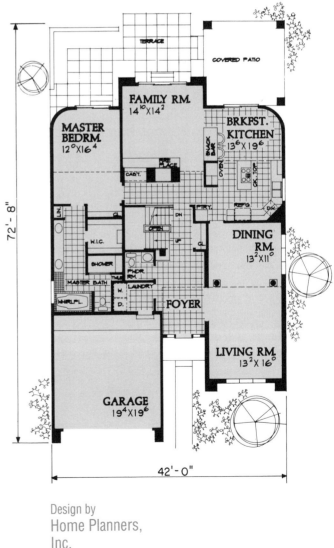

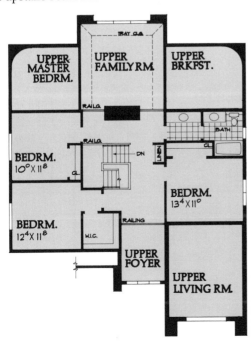

Design by
Home Planners,
Inc.

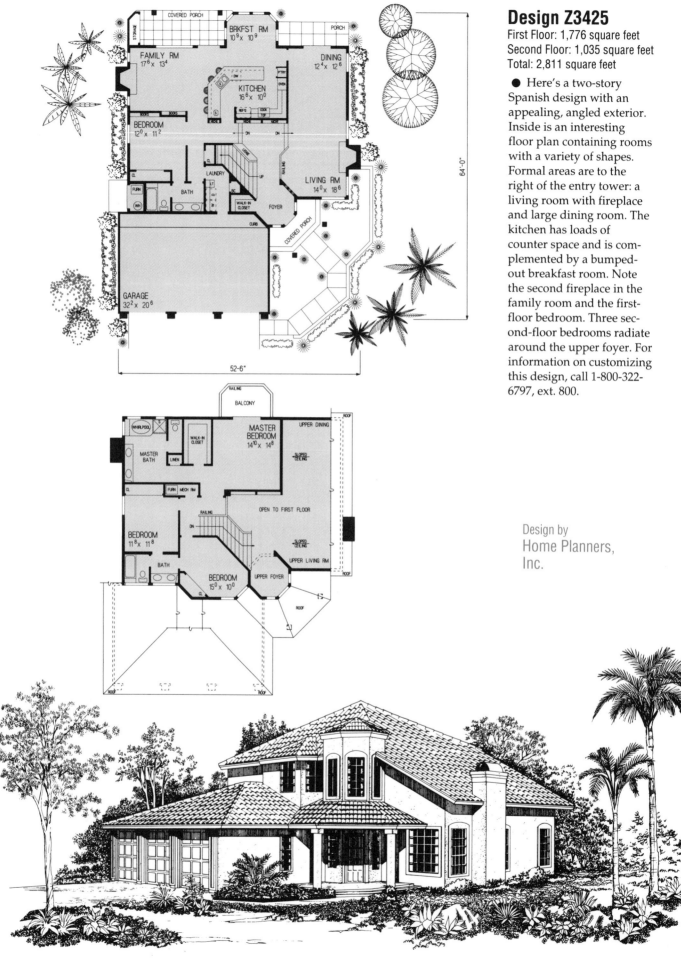

Design Z3425

First Floor: 1,776 square feet
Second Floor: 1,035 square feet
Total: 2,811 square feet

● Here's a two-story Spanish design with an appealing, angled exterior. Inside is an interesting floor plan containing rooms with a variety of shapes. Formal areas are to the right of the entry tower: a living room with fireplace and large dining room. The kitchen has loads of counter space and is complemented by a bumped-out breakfast room. Note the second fireplace in the family room and the first-floor bedroom. Three second-floor bedrooms radiate around the upper foyer. For information on customizing this design, call 1-800-322-6797, ext. 800.

Design by
Home Planners,
Inc.

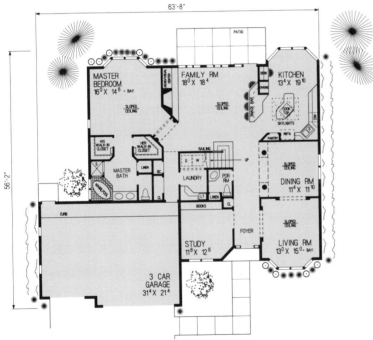

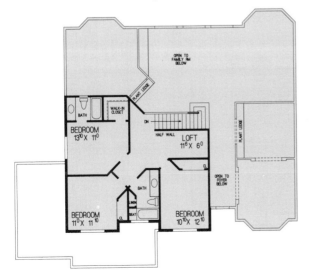

Design Z3441

First Floor: 2,022 square feet
Second Floor: 845 square feet
Total: 2,867 square feet

● Special details make the difference between a house and a home. A snack bar, audio/visual center and a fireplace make the family room livable. A desk, island cook top, bay, and skylights enhance the kitchen area. The dining room features two columns and a plant ledge. The first-floor master suite includes His and Hers walk-in closets, a spacious bath, and a bay window. On the second floor, one bedroom features a walk-in closet and private bath, while two additional bedrooms share a full bath. For information on customizing this design, call 1-800-322-6797, ext. 800.

Design by
Home Planners,
Inc.

167

● This uniquely Florida design brings all of the major living areas to the rear for extended outdoor livability. The separation of formal living areas adds excitement to dinner parties. The sunken living room leads to the patio. The kitchen with planning desk is convenient to the family room with fireplace, breakfast room and dining room. The coffered ceiling in the sunken dining room is an example of the unique detail in this design. The master suite includes a bath fit for a king: two walk-in closets, dual vanities, whirlpool tub and shower. The second floor houses three more bedrooms, one with a sitting room.

Design Z8650

First Floor: 1,828 square feet
Second Floor: 906 square feet
Total: 2,734 square feet

WIDTH 67'-4"
DEPTH 59'-8"

Design by
Home Design
Services, Inc.

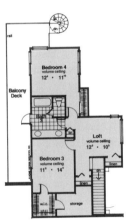

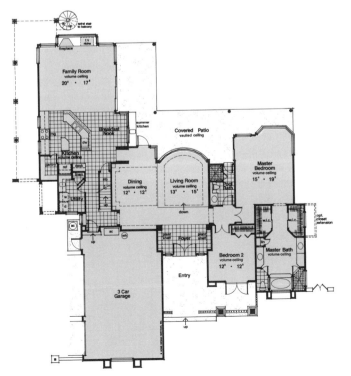

Design Z8656

First Floor: 2,515 square feet
Second Floor: 697 square feet
Total: 3,212 square feet

● This Mediterranean home is designed to function well on a golf course or near a lake, mountains or coastline. All of the living areas, including the dining room, are situated to the rear of the home. Mitered glass in the master bedroom and living areas brings wonderful vistas inside. A mitered bow window in the sunken living room is evidence of the design technology of the 1990s. The family room measures 17 x 20 feet and features a fireplace and built-in TV niche. The master suite, with its spacious bath, provides the ultimate in luxury. Two bedrooms on the second floor have access to the back yard by way of their own spiral stair. A loft area with two linen closets and a balcony round out the second floor.

WIDTH 70'-8"
DEPTH 84'-4"

Design by
Home Design
Services, Inc.

Design Z8655

First Floor: 2,624 square feet
Second Floor: 540 square feet
Total: 3,164 square feet

● This award-winning design has been recognized for its innovative use of spaces while continuing to keep family living spaces combined for maximum enjoyment. The formal spaces separate the master suite and den/study from family spaces. A convenient bath with outside access turns the den/study into a guest bedroom when needed. The master's retreat is generously supplied with space and contains a master bath with His and Hers vanities, private toilet room and walk-in closet. The perfect touch in this two-story design is the placement of three bedrooms downstairs with two extra bedrooms on the second floor. Study space on this floor overlooks the rooms below.

Design by
Home Design
Services, Inc.

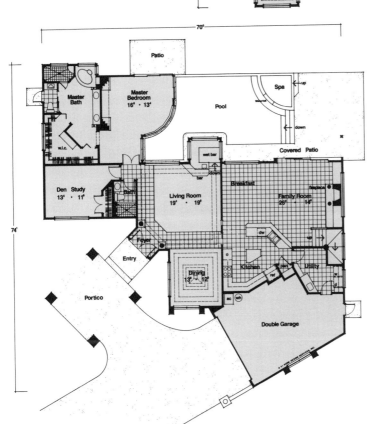

Design Z8652

First Floor: 2,212 square feet
Second Floor: 675 square feet
Total: 2,887 square feet

● As you drive up to the porte cochere entry of this home, the visual movement of the elevation is breathtaking. The multi-roofed spaces bring excitement the moment you walk through the double-doored entry. The foyer leads into the wide glass-walled living room. To the right, the formal dining room features a tiered pedestal ceiling. To the left is the guest and master suite wing of the home. The master suite with its sweeping curved glass wall has access to the patio area. The master bath, with its huge walk-in closet, comes complete with a columned vanity area, soaking tub and shower for two. Two large bedrooms on the second floor share a sun deck and an activity area.

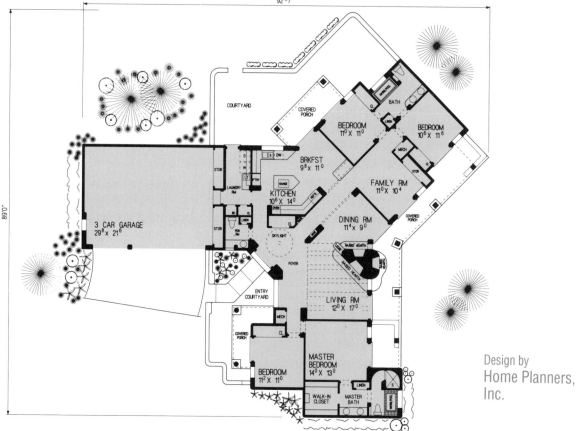

Design Z3433
Square Footage: 2,350

● Santa Fe styling creates interesting angles in this one-story home. A grand entrance leads through a courtyard into the foyer with circular skylight, closet space and niches, and convenient powder room. Turn right to the master suite with deluxe bath and a bedroom close at hand, perfect for a nursery, home office or exercise room. Two more family bedrooms are placed quietly in the far wing of the house. Fireplaces in the living room, dining room and covered porch create various shapes. Make note of the island range in the kitchen, extra storage in the garage, and covered porches on two sides. For information on customizing this design, call 1-800-322-6797, ext. 800.

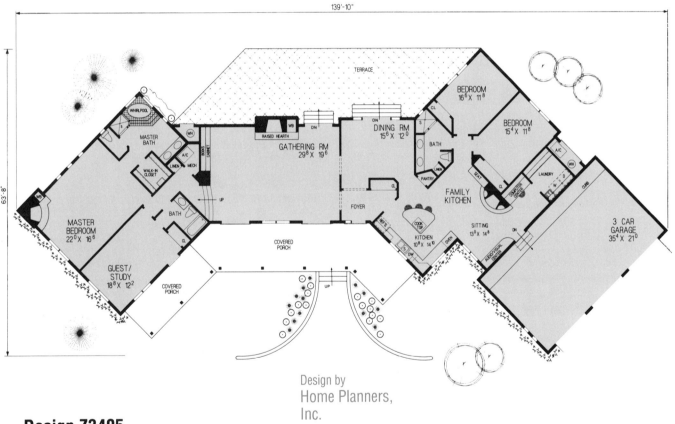

Design by
Home Planners,
Inc.

Design Z3405
Square Footage: 3,144

● In classic Santa Fe style, this home strikes a beautiful combination of historic exterior detailing and open floor planning on the inside. A covered porch running the width of the facade leads to an entry foyer that connects to a huge gathering room with fireplace and formal dining room. The family kitchen allows special space for casual gatherings. The right wing of the home holds two family bedrooms and full bath. The left wing is devoted to the master suite and guest room or study. For information on customizing this design, call 1-800-322-6797, ext. 800.

Design Z3435

First Floor: 1,946 square feet
Second Floor: 986 square feet
Total: 2,932 square feet

● Here's a grand Spanish Mission home designed for family living. Enter at the angled foyer which contains a curved staircase to the second floor. Family bedrooms are here along with a spacious guest suite. The master bedroom is found on the first floor and has a private patio and whirlpool overlooking an enclosed garden area. Besides a living room and dining room connected by a through-fireplace, there is a family room with casual eating space. There is also a library with large closet. You'll appreciate the abundant built-ins and interesting shapes throughout this home. For information on customizing this design, call 1-800-322-6797, ext. 800.

Design by
Home Planners,
Inc.

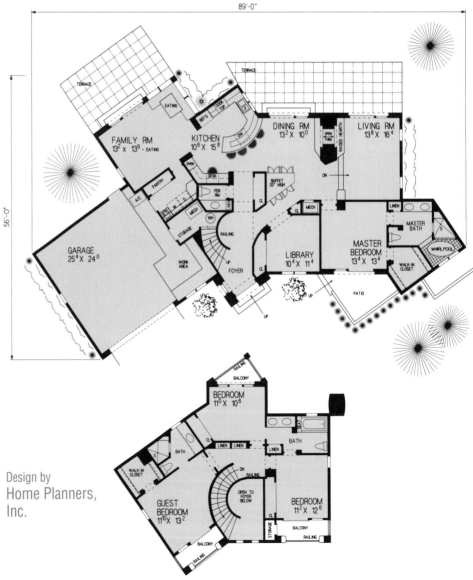

Transitional Home Plans

Combining the best of the old with the new, transitional home plans use traditional details and modern building techniques to create unique homes with a style all their own.

Exterior styles range from traditional to contemporary to Southwestern. Asymmetrical proportions, varied building materials, projecting garages and multi-gabled or hipped roofs are common characteristics of transitional homes. Large windows, two-story entryways and hipped roofs give these homes a volume look.

The designs on pages 176-179 feature horizontal wood siding on a traditional exterior with modern window treatment. Each design has four or five bedrooms plus a large bonus room over the garage.

Charming exteriors with stone accents highlight the homes on pages 186-190. Design Z9833 on page 187 has the look of a country manor, while Design Z3319 on page 190 combines all the best characteristics of bungalow and contemporary styles.

Rounding out this selection of transitional homes is a group of designs in what may be called "Florida" style. Hipped roofs, stucco exteriors, large window areas and covered patios are characteristics common to these designs.

Design Z9515

First Floor: 1,281 square feet
Second Floor: 1,257 square feet
Total: 2,538 square feet

● This five-bedroom home accommodates the large family with ease. An efficient floor plan places formal areas to the right. The living room features a fireplace and is open to the dining room. The kitchen offers an island cooktop, a pantry, a built-in desk and an adjacent breakfast nook with double doors to the rear yard. The light-infused family room features sliding glass doors and a second fireplace. The master bedroom includes a spacious bath with spa tub, separate shower, dual vanities, linen storage and a large closet. Bedroom 5, to the front of the home, can function alternatively as a den with a built-in cabinet.

Design by
Alan Mascord
Design Associates, Inc.

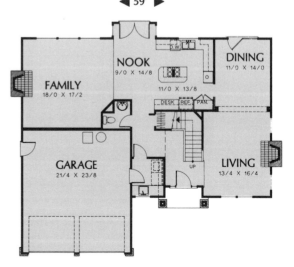

Design Z9477

First Floor: 1,308 square feet
Second Floor: 1,141 square feet
Total: 2,449 square feet

Design by
Alan Mascord
Design Associates, Inc.

◀ 56' ▶

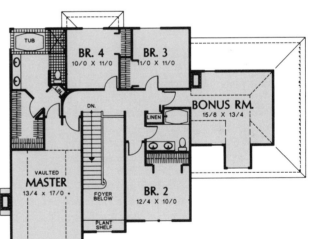

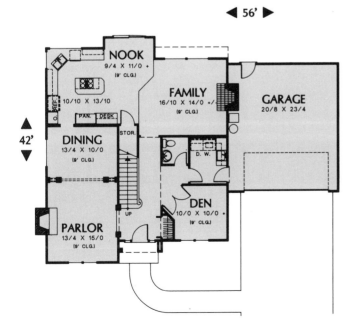

● Quietly stated elegance is the key to this home's attraction. Its floor plan allows plenty of space for formal and informal occasions. Note that the rear of the first floor is devoted to an open area serving as family room, breakfast nook and island kitchen. This area is comple-mented by a formal parlor/dining room combi-nation. A private den could function as a guest room with the handy powder room nearby. There are four bedrooms on the second floor. Bonus room over the garage could become an additional bedroom or study.

Design Z9504

First Floor: 1,465 square feet
Second Floor: 1,103 square feet
Total: 2,568 square feet
Bonus Room: 303 square feet

● With a plan that boasts excellent traffic patterns, this home will accommodate the modern family well. A spacious foyer with a plant shelf and elegant staircase greets visitors. Formal dining and living rooms remain to one side of the house and create an elegant atmosphere for entertaining. Highlights of the front den include a bay window and built-in bookshelves. The gourmet kitchen opens into a nook and a family room with a fireplace. A convenient utility room offers passage to the three-car garage. Three bedrooms, including a spacious master suite, and a bonus room—perfect for a gameroom—constitute the second floor.

Design by
Alan Mascord
Design Associates, Inc.

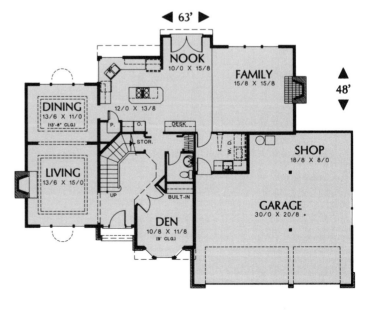

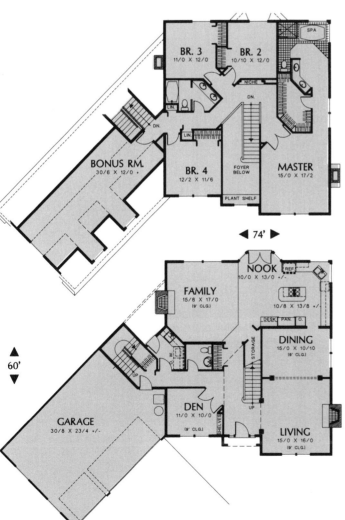

◀ 74' ▶

▲
60'
▼

Design Z9514

First Floor: 1,620 square feet
Second Floor: 1,331 square feet
Total: 2,951 square feet
Bonus Room: 486 square feet

● A striking facade opens to an impressive two-story foyer with a plant shelf. The formal living room with a fireplace and the dining room are open to each other. To the left of the foyer is a den with built-in shelves. The kitchen features an island cooktop, a pantry and a built-in planning desk. It is convenient to the breakfast room with bay and the family room with another fireplace. Double doors open to the master suite with walk-in closet and bath with spa tub and dual vanities. Three family bedrooms share a compartmented bath. A 30-foot bonus room over the three-car garage is near a second stairway.

Design by
Alan Mascord
Design Associates, Inc.

179

Design by
Home Planners,
Inc.

Design Z3452

First Floor: 1,545 square feet
Second Floor: 805 square feet
Total: 2,350 square feet

● Clean lines and tasteful window treatment create a pleasing facade. The formal living room (with vaulted ceiling) and dining room are open to each other. To the right of the foyer is a parlor that may serve as a guest bedroom, with a full bath nearby. The island kitchen easily serves the octagonal breakfast room and the family room with a vaulted ceiling and a fireplace. A rear patio can be accessed from the family room or breakfast room. Two stairways lead to the second floor. Balconies overlook the living and family rooms. The master bedroom features a luxurious bath and a walk-in closet, while two family bedrooms share a full bath.

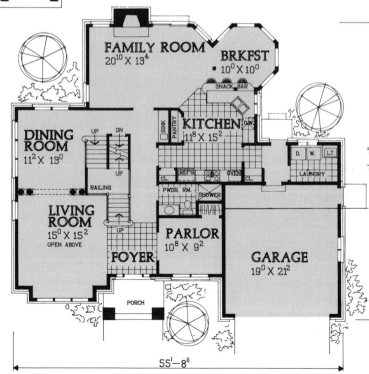

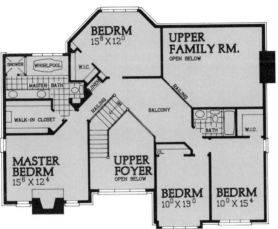

Design Z3446

First Floor: 1,532 square feet
Second Floor: 1,200 square feet
Total: 2,732 square feet

● A unique facade harbors a spacious, two-story foyer with an angled stairway. To the left is the formal living room with a fireplace and half walls separating the formal dining room. To the right is a quiet den. The kitchen and breakfast room combination takes advantage of a sunny bay. The family room features a second fireplace and a vaulted ceiling with three skylights. Yet another fireplace is found in the master bedroom suite, which includes a pampering master bath with walk-in closet, dual vanities and a separate tub and shower. Bedroom 2 is set into a bay and features a walk-in closet. Two additional family bedrooms and a full bath round out the second floor.

Design by
Home Planners,
Inc.

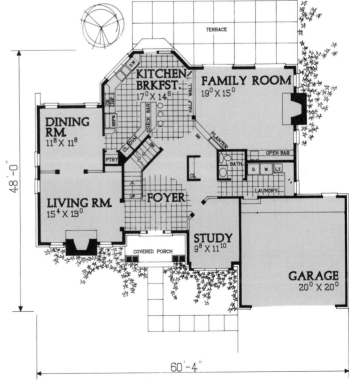

Design Z3450

First Floor: 1,801 square feet
Second Floor: 1,086 square feet
Total: 2,887 square feet

● A striking facade includes a covered front porch with four columns. To the left of the foyer is a large gathering room with a fireplace and bay window. The adjoining dining room leads to a covered side porch. The kitchen includes a snack bar, pantry, desk, and eating area. The first-floor master suite provides a spacious bath with walk-in closet, whirlpool and shower. Also on the first floor: a study and a garage workshop. Two bedrooms and a lavish guest suite share the second floor. For information on customizing this design, call 1-800-322-6797, ext. 800.

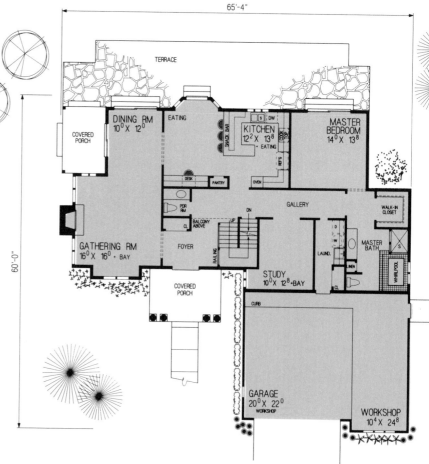

Design by
Home Planners,
Inc.

Design Z3439

First Floor: 1,425 square feet
Second Floor: 989 square feet
Total: 2,414 square feet

● Featuring a facade of wood and window glass, this home presents a striking first impression. It's floor plan is equally as splendid. Formal living and dining areas flank the entry foyer—both are sunken two steps down. Also sunken from the foyer is the family room with attached breakfast nook. A fireplace in this area sits adjacent to a built-in audio-visual center. A nearby study with adjacent full bath doubles as a guest room. Upstairs are three bedrooms including a master suite with whirlpool spa and walk-in closet. Plant shelves adorn the entire floor plan. For information on customizing this design, call 1-800-322-6797, ext. 800.

65'-2"

52'-10"

TERRACE

FAMILY RM
12² X 18⁶

NOOK
14² X 8⁰

STUDY
12⁰ X 12⁰

AUDIO/VISUAL CENTER

VAULTED CEILING

LINE OF FLOOR ABOVE

SLOPED ROOF WINDOWS ABOVE

KITCHEN
12⁶ X 12⁰

DW

S

REF'S

COOK TOP

PLANT SHELVES ABOVE

BUTLER'S PANTRY

D

BATH

W

PTRY

LINEN

LAUNDRY

BC

DN

UP

VAULTED CEILING

CL

DN

FOYER

DN

VAULTED CEILING

DINING RM
9⁸ X 11⁸

LIVING RM
12² X 12²

COVERED PORCH

2 CAR GARAGE
14¹⁰ X 16⁴

Design by
Home Planners,
Inc.

OPEN TO FAMILY RM BELOW

PLANT SHELF

BEDROOM
11⁶ X 10⁶

CL

BATH

LINEN

DN

RAILING

BALCONY

BEDROOM
10⁶ X 10⁴

CL

OPEN TO FOYER BELOW

OPEN TO DINING RM BELOW

RAILING

NICHE

MASTER BEDROOM
13⁰ X 14⁰

PLANT SHELF

S

SEAT

MASTER BATH

WHIRLPOOL

PLANT SHELF

WALK-IN CLOSET

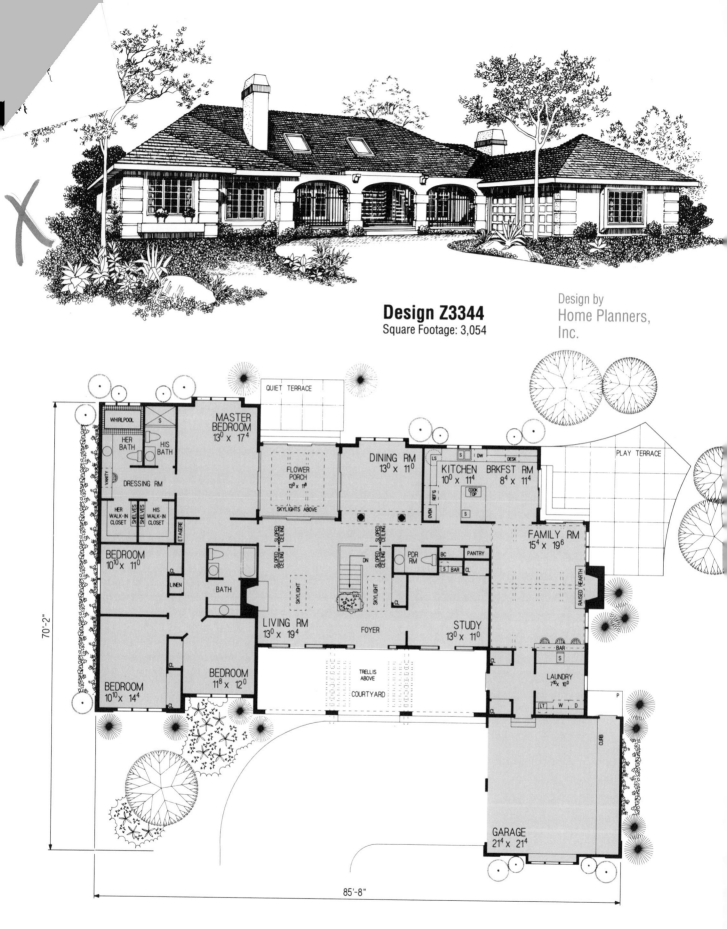

Design Z3344
Square Footage: 3,054

Design by
Home Planners,
Inc.

● This home features interior planning for today's active family. Living areas include a living room with fireplace, a cozy study and family room with wet bar. Convenient to the kitchen is the formal dining room with attractive bay window overlooking the back yard. The four-bedroom sleeping area contains a sumptuous master suite. Also notice the cheerful flower porch with access from the master suite, living room and dining room.

Design Z3565

First Floor: 1,248 square feet
Second Floor: 1,012 square feet
Total: 2,260 square feet

● Every detail of this plan
speaks of modern design. The
exterior is simple yet elegant,
while interior floor planning is
thorough yet efficient. The formal living and dining rooms are
to the left of the home, separated by columns. The living room
features a wall of windows and
a fireplace. The kitchen with
island cooktop is adjacent to the
large family room with terrace
access. A study with additional
terrace access completes the first
floor. The master bedroom features a balcony and a spectacular bath with whirlpool tub,
shower with seat, separate vanities and a walk-in closet. Two
family bedrooms share access to
a full bath. Also notice the three-
car garage.

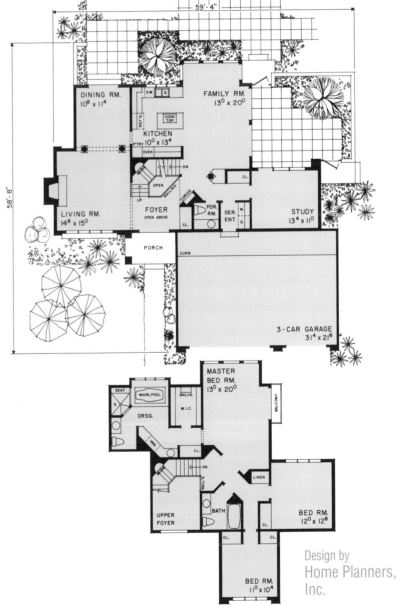

Design by
Home Planners,
Inc.

Design Z9821

First Floor: 2,070 square feet
Second Floor: 790 square feet
Total: 2,860 square feet

Design by
Design Traditions

● The striking combination of wood frame, shingles and glass create the exterior of this classic cottage. The foyer opens to the main level layout. To the left of the foyer is a study with a warming hearth and vaulted ceiling. To the right is the formal dining room. A great room with attached breakfast area is to the rear near the

kitchen. A guest room is nestled in the rear of the plan for privacy. The master suite provides an expansive tray ceiling, glass sitting area and easy passage to the outside deck. Upstairs, two bedrooms are accompanied by a loft for a quiet getaway.

WIDTH 57'-6"
DEPTH 54'

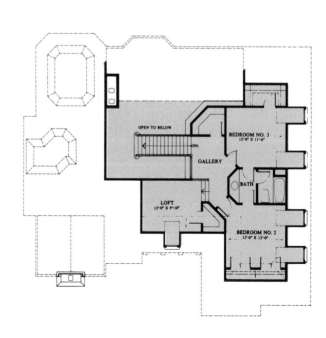

Design Z9833

First Floor: 1,683 square feet
Second Floor: 1,544 square feet
Total: 3,227 square feet

● Handsomely arranged, this Country Cottage possesses an inviting quality. The stucco exterior, mixed with stone and shingles, creates a warmth that is accented with a fan-light transom and pendant door frame. The formal two-story foyer opens onto all the drama of the staircase and then flows easily into the dining room, living room and great room. The great room features a fireplace and bookcases on the side wall and opens to a well-lit breakfast and kitchen area. To complete the main level of this home, a guest room or office is planned, offering visitors the utmost in privacy. Provided upstairs are three additional bedrooms and space for a bonus or play room. The master suite features a tray ceiling and adjoining sitting area with special ceiling treatment. The master bath offers a large garden tub with separate vanities, His and Hers closets and an octagonal glass shower.

Design by
Design Traditions

187

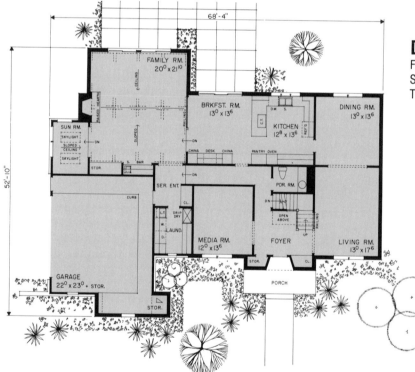

Design Z3370

First Floor: 2,055 square feet
Second Floor: 1,288 square feet
Total: 3,343 square feet

Design by
Home Planners,
Inc.

● The combination of stone and brick creates an impressive facade on this traditional two-story. The symmetrically designed interior will provide efficient traffic patterns. Note the formal living and dining areas to the right and huge family room to the rear. The U-shaped kitchen has an attached breakfast room and built-ins. There are four bedrooms on the second floor. The master features a walk-in closet, double vanity and whirlpool tub.

Design Z3356

First Floor: 1,610 square feet
Second Floor: 1,200 square feet
Total: 2,810 square feet

● Traditionally speaking, this home takes blue ribbons. Its family room has a raised-hearth fireplace and there's a covered porch reached through sliding glass doors for informal eating. The living room also has a fireplace and is near the boxed-windowed dining room. A large clutter room off the garage could be turned into a hobby or sewing room. Four bedrooms on the second floor include a master suite with His and Hers walk-in closets and three family bedrooms.

Design by
Home Planners,
Inc.

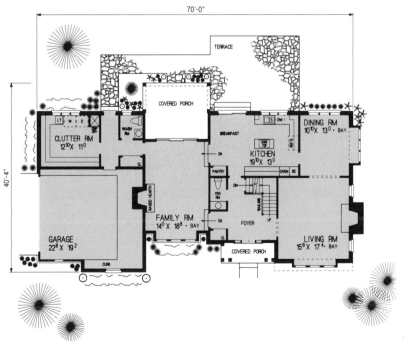

Design Z3319

Square Footage: 2,274

● This attractive bungalow design separates the master suite from family bedrooms and puts casual living to the back in a family room. The formal living and dining areas are centrally located and have access to a rear terrace, as does the master suite. The kitchen sits between formal and informal living areas. The two family bedrooms are found to the front of the plan. A home office or study opens off the front foyer and the master suite. For information on customizing this design, call 1-800-322-6797, ext. 800.

Design by
Home Planners,
Inc.

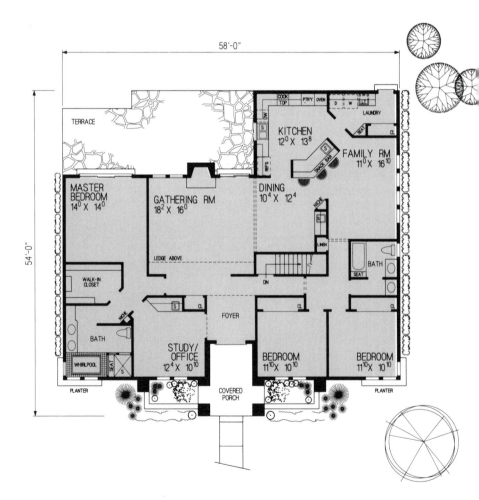

58'-0"

54'-0"

TERRACE

KITCHEN
12⁰ X 13⁸

LAUNDRY

FAMILY RM
11⁰ X 16¹⁰

MASTER BEDROOM
14⁰ X 14⁰

GATHERING RM
18² X 16⁰

DINING
10⁴ X 12⁴

LEDGE ABOVE

LINEN

BATH

WALK-IN CLOSET

DN

FOYER

BATH

STUDY/ OFFICE
12⁴ X 10¹⁰

BEDROOM
11¹⁰ X 10¹⁰

BEDROOM
11¹⁰ X 10¹⁰

WHIRLPOOL

PLANTER

COVERED PORCH

PLANTER

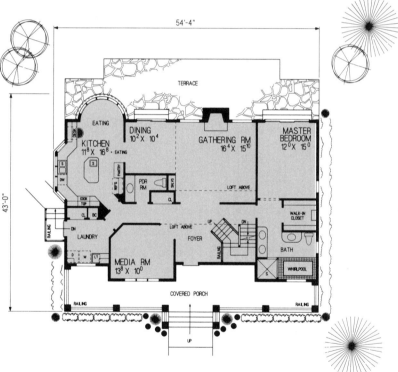

TERRACE

EATING

KITCHEN
11⁸ X 16⁸ · EATING

DINING
10² X 10⁴

GATHERING RM
16⁴ X 15¹⁰

MASTER
BEDROOM
12⁰ X 15⁰

PDR
RM

LOFT ABOVE

CL

WALK-IN
CLOSET

COOK
TOP

CL

BC

LOFT ABOVE

UP

DN

RAILING

LAUNDRY

MEDIA RM
13⁸ X 10⁰

FOYER

RAILING

BATH

WHIRLPOOL

COVERED PORCH

RAILING

RAILING

UP

54'-4"

43'-0"

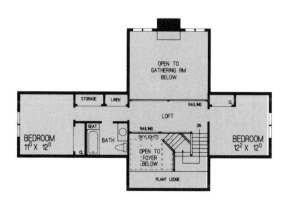

OPEN TO
GATHERING RM
BELOW

STORAGE   LINEN

RAILING

CL

LOFT

BEDROOM
11⁰ X 12⁰

SEAT

BATH

CL

RAILING

SKYLIGHTS

OPEN TO
FOYER
BELOW

DN

BEDROOM
12² X 12⁰

PLANT LEDGE

Design Z3321

First Floor: 1,636 square feet
Second Floor: 572 square feet
Total: 2,208 square feet

● Cozy and completely functional, this 1½-story bungalow has many amenities not often found in homes its size. The covered porch at the front opens at the entry to a foyer with angled staircase. To the left is a media room, to the rear the gathering room with fireplace. Attached to the gathering room is a formal dining room with rear terrace access. The kitchen features a curved casual eating area and island work station. The right side of the first floor is dominated by the master suite. It has access to the rear terrace and a luxurious bath. Upstairs are two family bedrooms connected by a loft area overlooking the gathering room and foyer. For information on customizing this design, call 1-800-322-6797, ext. 800.

Design by
Home Planners,
Inc.

Design Z9281 First Floor: 1,697 square feet
Second Floor: 694 square feet; Total: 2,391 square feet

● Arched transom windows plus the combination of siding and brick create the magic of this four-bedroom, 1½-story home. French doors lead into the volume living room with arched window. To the right, a hutch space adds to the versatility of the dining room. Casual traffic patterns start with the large great room with a two-sided fireplace and windows out the back. A walk-in pantry, desk and island in the kitchen opens to a semi-gazebo dinette. Don't miss the luxurious master dressing/bath area featuring His and Hers vanities, a walk-in closet and a corner whirlpool. Each secondary bedroom upstairs benefits from a built-in desk and a shared, compartmented bath.

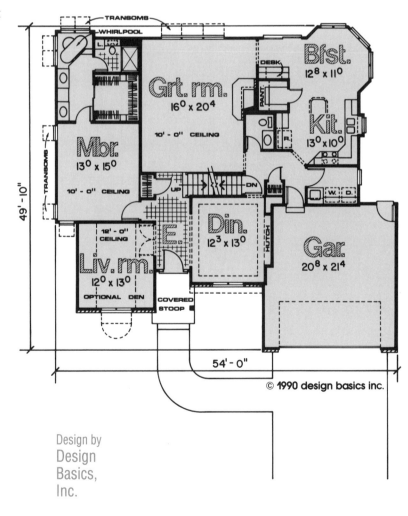

© 1990 design basics inc.

Design by
Design Basics, Inc.

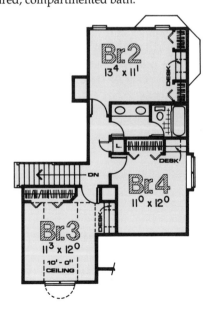

Design Z9369

First Floor: 1,369 square feet
Second Floor: 1,111 square feet
Total: 2,480 square feet

● Combined dining and living areas (with ten-foot ceilings) provide abundant space for formal entertaining or holiday gatherings. Or if preferred, escape to the den for quiet time with a book—built-in bookshelves fill out one wall of this room. The kitchen makes use of island counter space and a breakfast nook. The large family room with fireplace and beamed ceiling, laundry and powder room round out the first floor. The garage accommodates three cars. The master bedroom—with tiered ceiling and bath with whirlpool—highlights the second floor. Three additional bedrooms and another full bath serve to complete the design.

Design by
Design
Basics,
Inc.

© design basics inc. 1991

Design Z8607

Square Footage: 2,271

● The family room, with volume ceiling, serves as a hub in this spacious home. It blends with a large covered patio to form an expansive, informal space. Special amenities here include a fireplace and sliding glass doors. The high ceiling extends to the kitchen and beyond to the bayed breakfast nook. A pass-through counter permits easy access between the kitchen and family room. The master bedroom is highlighted by a volume ceiling and patio access. A tiled shower and step-up tub in the master bath overlook the solarium. Three additional bedrooms, two flanking a tiled bath, are found beyond the living room. A third bedroom is located off the family room and features its own private bath. This plan includes a slab foundation.

WIDTH 63'
DEPTH 51'-4"

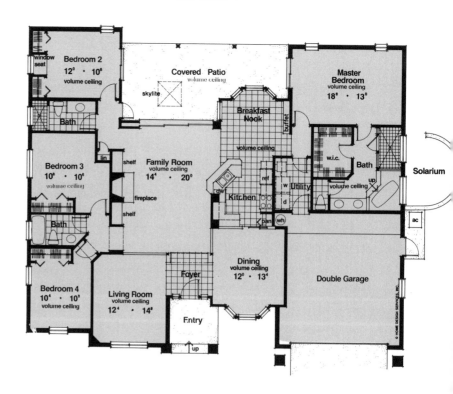

Design by
Home Design
Services, Inc.

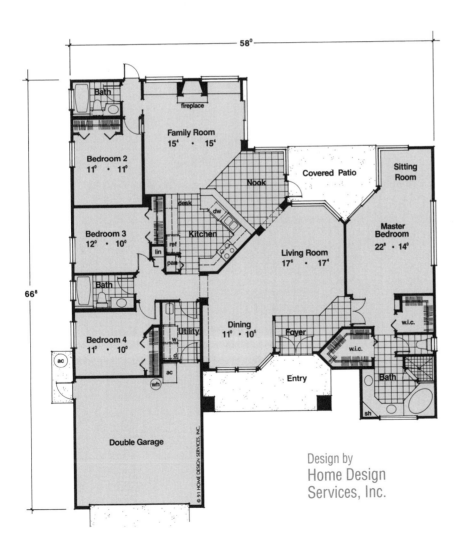

Design Z8641
Square Footage: 2,253

● The functional use of angles in this house make for a plan which is exciting and full of large spaces. A formal living/dining area greets guests as they enter. The mitered glass throughout the rear of the home creates unlimited views to the outdoor living space and pool. Double doors lead to the master suite. A grand bath here boasts His and Hers walk-in closets, a wraparound vanity, a corner tub and a shower. The best feature of this home is the split-bedroom design. It contains a bedroom that has a private bath, perfect for guest or family member visits. The remaining two bedrooms share their own bath off the hall.

Design by
Home Design
Services, Inc.

Design Z8627

Square footage: 3,743

● A central foyer gives way to a spread-out design. Straight ahead, the living room features French doors set in a bay area. To the left, columns and a coffered ceiling offset the exquisite formal dining room. A fireplace warms the expansive family room which adjoins the breakfast nook. Traffic flows easily through the ample kitchen with cooktop island and pass-through to the patio. The master bedroom features a tray ceiling, walk-in closet and sumptuous bath with shower and step-up tub overlooking a private garden. Two bedrooms are joined by an optional media room and optional study, which could bring the count up to five bedrooms if necessary.

Design by
Home Design
Services, Inc.

Contemporary Home Plans

Contemporary style had its beginnings in the 1950s, when American architects began to create houses with sleeker lines and fewer exterior features. Building upon the earlier work of Frank Lloyd Wright, Louis Sullivan, Charles and Henry Greene and other innovative architects, they designed houses to blend into the landscape and integrate indoor and outdoor space. Traditional ornamentation on windows, doors and chimneys was missing.

A series of Southwestern contemporaries opens this diverse selection of designs. Curving lines and rounded edges give these stucco homes a distinctive appearance. Arched entryways, creative window treatment and glass block walls add architectural interest.

The most popular contemporary is a one-story house, although 1½-story, two-story and multi-level houses are frequently seen. Roofs are generally side- and cross-gabled with a low pitch, while flat or shed-style roofs are also common. Frank Lloyd Wright and other architects employed wide overhanging eaves, a feature exclusive to contemporary style. Exteriors vary from region to region, with stucco popular in the Southwest, vertical wood siding in the Pacific Northwest and combinations of wall materials seen in all areas.

Contemporary homes make the most of outdoor areas through the use of large windows, sliding glass doors, skylights, balconies, patios, decks and terraces. Take special note of the decks on Design Z2511 and Design Z2937 on pages 206 and 207.

Design Z3403

First Floor: 2,240 square feet
Second Floor: 660 square feet
Total: 2,900 square feet

Design by
Home Planners,
Inc.

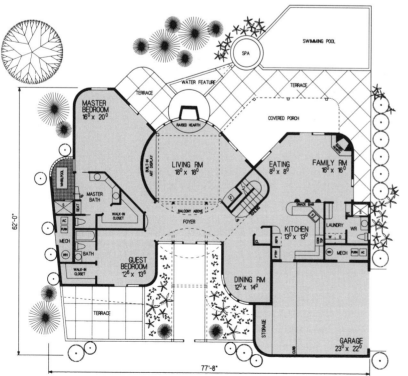

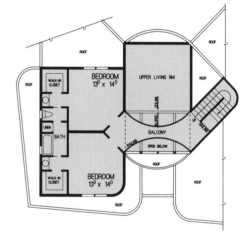

● There is no end to the distinctive features in this Southwestern contemporary. Formal living areas are concentrated in the center of the plan, perfect for entertaining. To the right of the plan, the kitchen and family room function well together as a working and living area. Also note the separate laundry room. The optional guest bedroom or den and the master bedroom are located to the left of the plan. Upstairs, the remaining two bedrooms are reached by a balcony overlooking the living room and share a bath with twin vanities.

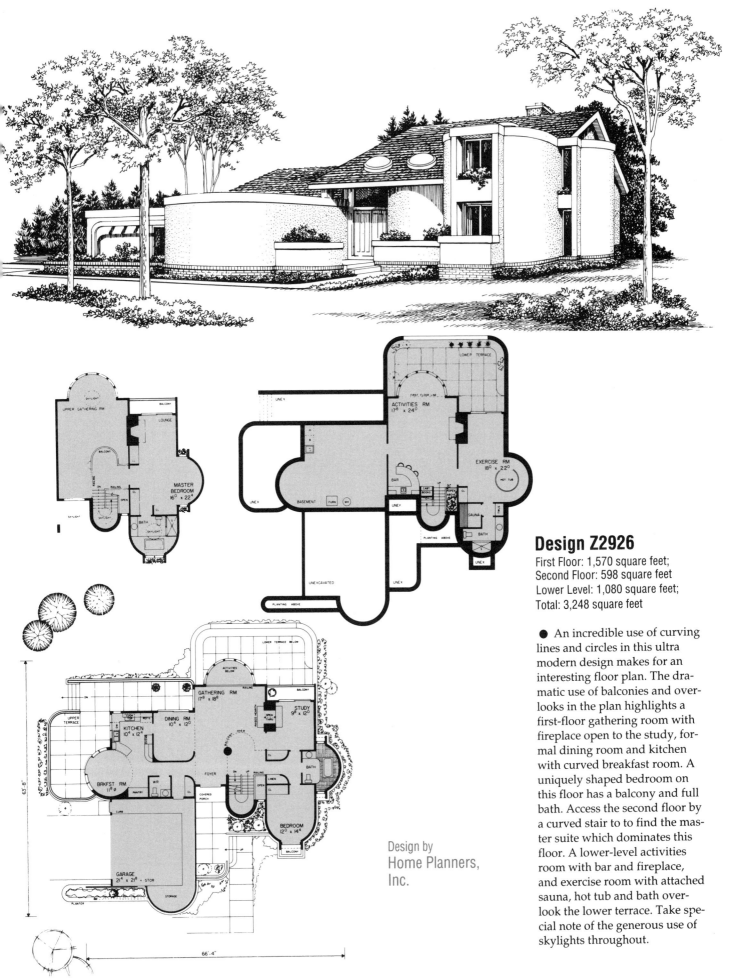

Design Z2926

First Floor: 1,570 square feet;
Second Floor: 598 square feet
Lower Level: 1,080 square feet;
Total: 3,248 square feet

● An incredible use of curving lines and circles in this ultra modern design makes for an interesting floor plan. The dramatic use of balconies and over-looks in the plan highlights a first-floor gathering room with fireplace open to the study, formal dining room and kitchen with curved breakfast room. A uniquely shaped bedroom on this floor has a balcony and full bath. Access the second floor by a curved stair to to find the master suite which dominates this floor. A lower-level activities room with bar and fireplace, and exercise room with attached sauna, hot tub and bath over-look the lower terrace. Take special note of the generous use of skylights throughout.

Design by
Home Planners,
Inc.

199

Design Z3408

Square Footage: 2,406

● Interesting angles make for interesting rooms. The sleeping zone features two large bedrooms with unique shapes and a master suite with spectacular bath. A laundry placed nearby is both convenient and economical, located adjacent to a full bath. The central kitchen offers a desk and built-in breakfast table. Meals can also be enjoyed in the adjacent eating area, formal dining room with stepped ceiling, or outside on the rear patio. A planter and glass block wall separate the living room and family room, which is warmed by a fireplace.

Design by
Home Planners,
Inc.

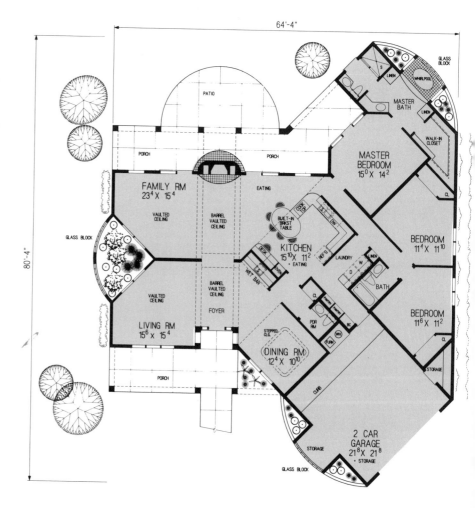

Design Z3409

First Floor: 1,481 square feet
Second Floor: 1,287 square feet
Total: 2,768 square feet

● Glass block walls and a foyer with barrel vaulted ceiling create an interesting exterior. Covered porches to the front and rear provide for excellent indoor/outdoor living relationships. Inside, a large planter and through-fireplace enhance the living room and family room. The dining room has a stepped ceiling. A desk, eating area and snack bar are special features in the kitchen. The master suite features a large walk-in closet, bath with double bowl vanity and separate tub and shower, and a private deck. Three additional bedrooms share a full bath.

Design by
Home Planners,
Inc.

Design Z9499

First Floor: 1,762 square feet
Second Floor: 1,233 square feet
Total: 2,995 square feet

● This stucco contemporary plan is resplendent and quite distinct with wide eaves and inventive window design. The floor plan adds some unique touches as well. The entry foyer leads to a formal living room and dining room on the left and a den or music room on the right. The family room is to the back of the plan and contains a warming corner fireplace. The kitchen is quite different--it boasts a two-story ceiling and is overlooked by the balcony upstairs. Bedrooms include two family bedrooms with shared bath and a master suite. The master includes a private balcony and pampering bath. Cove ceilings can be found in the master suite and also in the dining room and living room.

Design by
Alan Mascord
Design Associates, Inc.

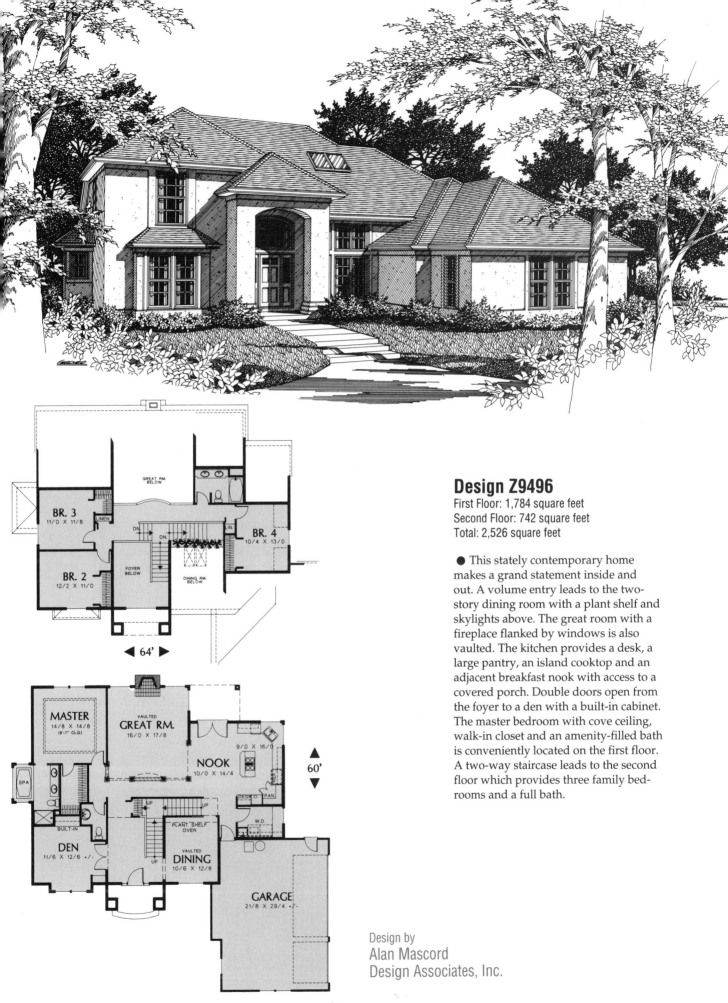

Design Z9496

First Floor: 1,784 square feet
Second Floor: 742 square feet
Total: 2,526 square feet

● This stately contemporary home
makes a grand statement inside and
out. A volume entry leads to the two-
story dining room with a plant shelf and
skylights above. The great room with a
fireplace flanked by windows is also
vaulted. The kitchen provides a desk, a
large pantry, an island cooktop and an
adjacent breakfast nook with access to a
covered porch. Double doors open from
the foyer to a den with a built-in cabinet.
The master bedroom with cove ceiling,
walk-in closet and an amenity-filled bath
is conveniently located on the first floor.
A two-way staircase leads to the second
floor which provides three family bedrooms and a full bath.

Design by
Alan Mascord
Design Associates, Inc.

Design Z9498

First Floor: 2,270 square feet
Second Floor: 788 square feet
Total: 3,058 square feet

● Dramatic on the highest level, this spectacular plan offers a recessed entry, double rows of multi-paned windows and two dormers over the garage. On the inside, formal living and dining areas reside to the right of the foyer and are separated from it by columns. A private den is also accessed from the foyer through double doors. The family room with fireplace is to the rear. It adjoins the breakfast nook and attached island kitchen. The master suite is on the first floor to separate it from family bedrooms. They are found on the second floor--there are two with the option of another. There are also two full baths on this floor. Bonus space over the garage can be developed at a later time.

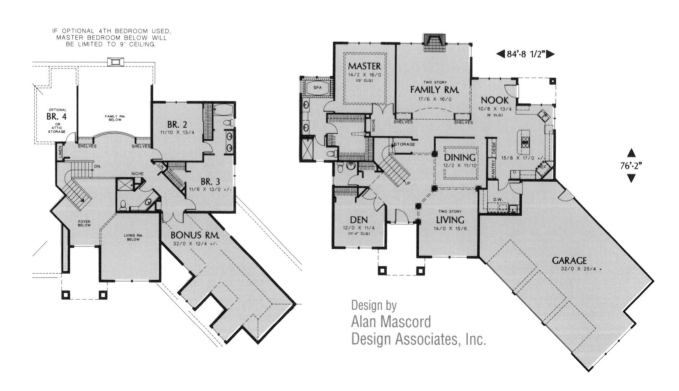

Design by
Alan Mascord
Design Associates, Inc.

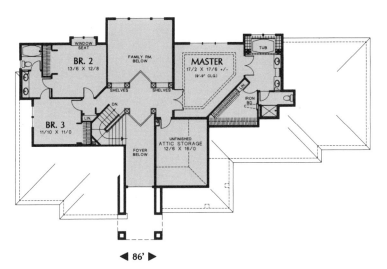

◀ 86' ▶

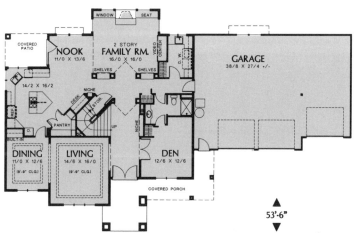

▲
53'-6"
▼

Design Z9512

First Floor: 1,797 square feet
Second Floor: 1,190 square feet
Total: 2,987 square feet

● This grand home presents a striking facade with a columned entrance and covered front porch. The living areas flow together for ease in entertaining. The living and dining rooms have tray ceilings. The kitchen is a cook's delight, with an island cooktop, huge pantry, planning desk and adjacent breakfast nook with access to a covered patio. A two-story family room includes built-in shelves, a built-in video center, window seats and an optional fireplace. A den to the front of the home provides a cozy retreat. A grand staircase leads to the second floor with three bedrooms and attic storage space. The master suite features a spacious bath with spa tub, His and Hers vanities and a walk-in closet with a built-in ironing board. Two family bedrooms share a Hollywood bath.

Design by
Alan Mascord
Design Associates, Inc.

Design Z2511

Main Level: 1,043 square feet
Upper Level: 703 square feet
Lower Level: 794 square feet
Total: 2,540 square feet

Design by
Home Planners,
Inc.

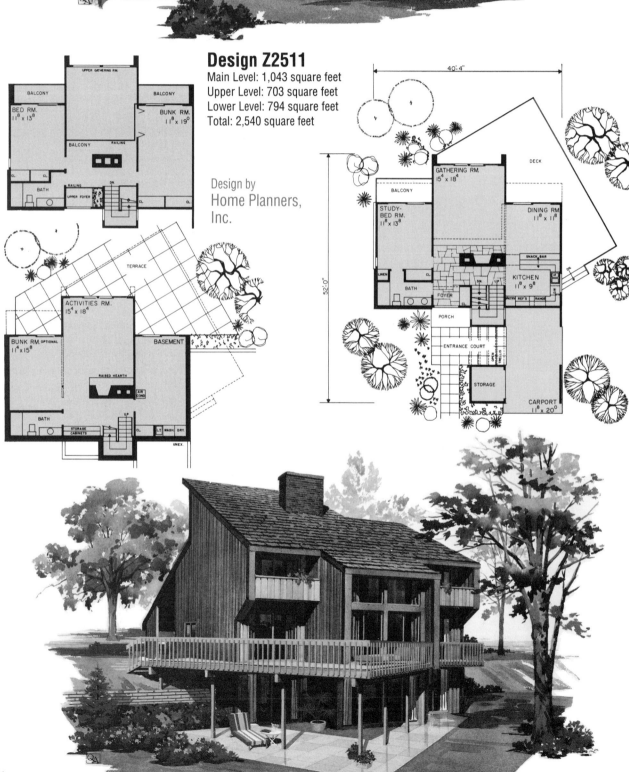

UPPER GATHERING RM.

BALCONY

BALCONY

BED RM.
11⁸ x 13⁸

BUNK RM.
11⁸ x 19⁰

BALCONY   RAILING

CL.   CL.

BATH   RAILING   UPPER FOYER   DN.   CL.   CL.

TERRACE

ACTIVITIES RM.
15⁴ x 18⁴

BUNK RM. OPTIONAL
11⁴ x15⁸

BASEMENT

RAISED HEARTH

AIR COND

BATH   STORAGE CABINETS   UP   CL.   LT   WASH. DRY.

UNEX.

40'- 4"

DECK

GATHERING RM.
15⁴ x 18⁴

BALCONY

STUDY-
BED RM.
11⁸ x 13⁸

DINING RM.
11⁸ x 11⁸

52'-0"

LINEN   CL.

BATH

SNACK BAR

KITCHEN
11⁸ x 9⁸

FOYER   DN.   UP   PNTRY REF'G   RANGE

CL.

PORCH

ENTRANCE COURT

STORAGE

CARPORT
11⁸ x 20⁰

Design Z2937

Main Level: 1,096 square feet; Upper Level: 1,115 square feet
Lower Level: 1,104 square feet; Total: 3,315 square feet

40'-0"

DECK

DECK

BALCONY
ABOVE

DINING RM.
13⁰ x 11⁸

GATHERING RM.
17⁸ x 15⁴

BRKFST. RM.
10⁸ x 14⁸

COOK TOP

KITCHEN
10⁸ x 11⁴

RAILING

56'-0"

DESK
CHINA

DN

OPEN ABOVE

RAILING

D W

CL

BRM PANTRY

FOYER

MUD RM.

WASH RM.

CL

COVERED PORCH

CURB

GARAGE
21⁴ x 21⁸

Design by
Home Planners, Inc.

TERRACE

TERRACE

HOBBIES
13⁰ x 11⁸

ACTIVITIES RM.
17⁰ x 15⁴

GUEST BEDROOM
11⁰ x 18⁸

MECH. RM.
9⁰ x 11⁴

LINEN

OPEN ABOVE

UP

BATH

CL

CL

UNEX

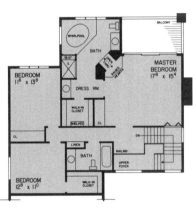

BALCONY

WHIRLPOOL

BATH

SEAT

MASTER BEDROOM
17⁸ x 15⁴

BEDROOM
11⁸ x 13⁸

DRESS. RM.

WALK-IN CLOSET

SHELVES

CL

LINEN

DN

CL

BATH

RAILING

UPPER FOYER

BEDROOM
12⁸ x 11⁰

WALK-IN CLOSET

207

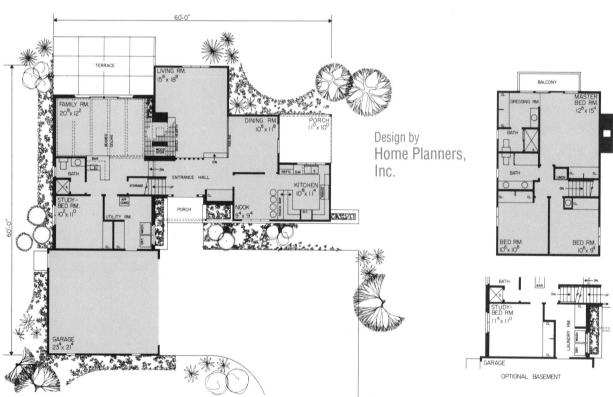

Design by
Home Planners,
Inc.

Design Z2379 First Floor: 1,525 square feet; Second Floor: 748 square feet; Total: 2,273 square feet

● A house that has "everything" may very well look just like this design. Its exterior is well-proportioned and impressive. Inside the inviting double front doors there are features galore. The living room and family room level is sunken. Separating these two rooms is a dramatic thru fireplace. A built-in bar, planter, and beamed ceiling highlight the family room. Nearby is a full bath and a study which could be utilized as a fourth bedroom. A fine functioning kitchen has a pass-thru to the snack bar of the breakfast nook. The adjacent dining room overlooks the living room and has sliding doors to the covered porch. Upstairs three bedrooms, two baths, and an outdoor balcony. Blueprints for this design include optional basement details. Laundry still remains on first floor.

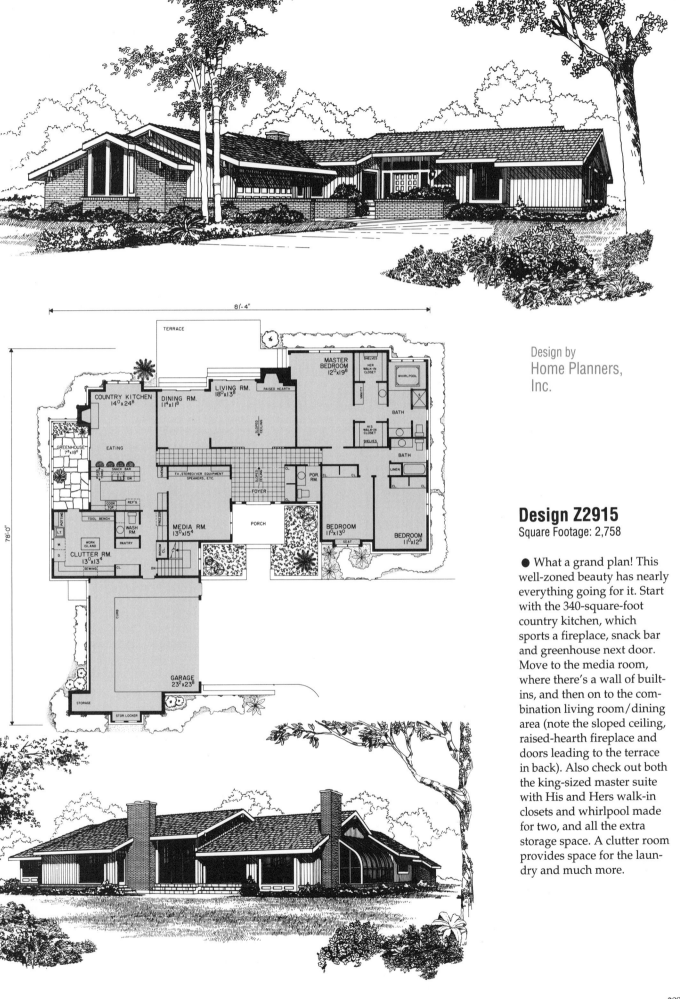

Design by
Home Planners,
Inc.

Design Z2915
Square Footage: 2,758

● What a grand plan! This well-zoned beauty has nearly everything going for it. Start with the 340-square-foot country kitchen, which sports a fireplace, snack bar and greenhouse next door. Move to the media room, where there's a wall of built-ins, and then on to the combination living room/dining area (note the sloped ceiling, raised-hearth fireplace and doors leading to the terrace in back). Also check out both the king-sized master suite with His and Hers walk-in closets and whirlpool made for two, and all the extra storage space. A clutter room provides space for the laundry and much more.

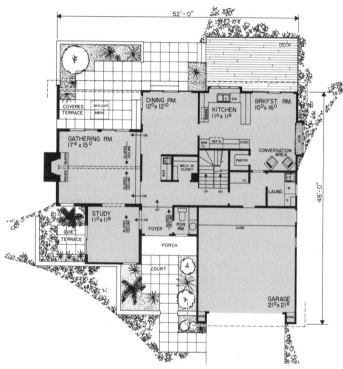

Design Z2823 First Floor: 1,370 square feet
Second Floor: 927 square feet; Total: 2,297 square feet

● The street view of this contemporary design features a small courtyard entrance as well as a private terrace off the study. Inside the livability will be outstanding. This design features spacious first-floor activity areas that flow smoothly into each other. In the gathering room a raised-hearth fireplace creates a dramatic focal point. An adjacent covered terrace, featuring a skylight, is ideal for outdoor dining and could be screened in later for an additional room.

Design by
Home Planners,
Inc.

Design by
Home Planners, Inc.

Design Z2781

First Floor: 2,132 square feet
Second Floor: 1,156 square feet
Total: 3,288 square feet

● This beautifully designed two-story could be con-
sidered a dream house of a
lifetime. The exterior is
sure to catch the eye of
anyone who takes sight of
its unique construction.
The front kitchen features
an island range, adjacent
breakfast nook and pass-
thru to formal dining room.
The master bedroom suite
with its privacy and con-
venience on the first floor
has a spacious walk-in
closet and dressing room.
The side terrace is accessible through sliding glass
doors from the master bedroom, gathering room and
study. The second floor has
three bedrooms and storage
space galore. Also notice
the lounge which has a
sloped ceiling and a sky-
light above. This delightful
area looks down into the
gathering room. The out-
door balconies overlook the
wrap-around terrace. Surely an outstanding trend
house for decades to come.

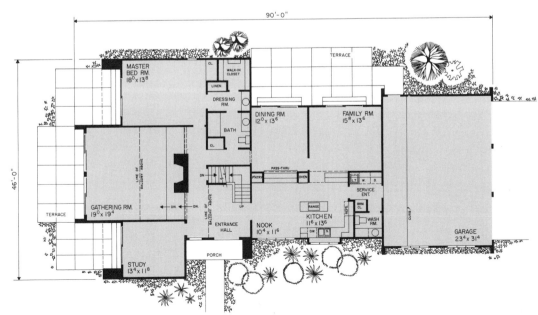

Design Z2858
Square Footage: 2,231

● This sun oriented design was created to face the south. By doing so, it has minimal northern exposure. It has been designed primarily for the more temperate U.S. latitudes using 2 x 6 wall construction. The morning sun will brighten the living and dining rooms along with the adjacent terrace. Sun enters the garden room by way of the glass roof and walls. In the winter, the solar heat gain from the garden room should provide relief from high energy bills. Solar shades allow you to adjust the amount of light that you want to enter in the warmer months. Interior planning deserves mention, too. The work center is efficient. The kitchen has a snack bar on the garden room side and a serving counter to the dining room. The breakfast room with laundry area is also convenient to the kitchen. Three bedrooms are on the northern wall. The master bedroom has a large tub and a separate shower with a four foot square skylight above. When this design is oriented toward the sun, it should prove to be energy efficient and a joy to live in.

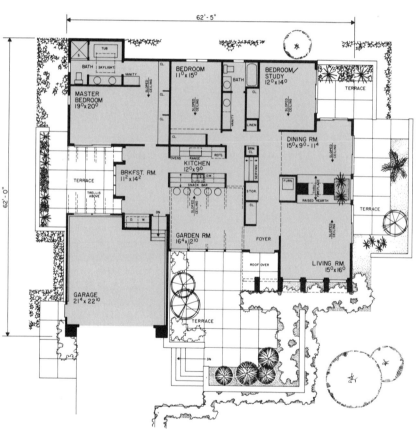

Design by
Home Planners,
Inc.

Design Z2832
Square Footage: 2,805 (Excluding Atrium)

● The advantage of passive solar heating is a significant highlight of this contemporary design. The huge skylight over the atrium provides shelter during inclement weather, while permitting natural light to enter below. The stone floor of this area absorbs an abundance of heat from the sun during the day and permits the circulation of warm air to other areas at night. Sloping ceilings highlight each of the major rooms: three bedrooms, formal living and dining rooms and the study. Broad expanses of roof can accommodate solar panels, if desired, to complement this design.

Design by
Home Planners,
Inc.

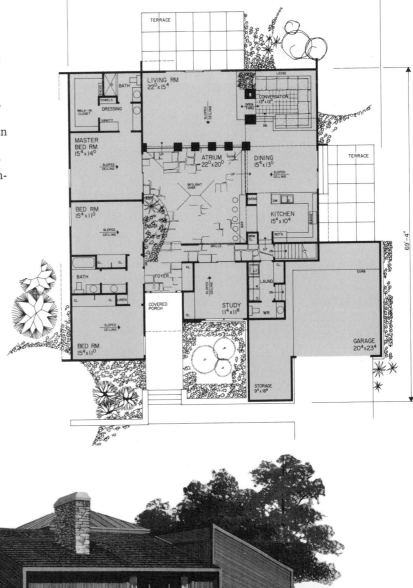

When You're Ready To Order . . .

Let Us Show You Our Home Blueprint Package.

Building a home? Planning a home? Our Blueprint Package contains nearly everything you need to get the job done right, whether you're working on your own or with help from an architect, designer, builder or subcontractors. Each Blueprint Package is the result of many hours of work by licensed architects or professional designers.

QUALITY

Hundreds of hours of painstaking effort have gone into the development of your blueprint set. Each home has been quality-checked by professionals to insure accuracy and buildability.

VALUE

Because we sell in volume, you can buy professional-quality blueprints at a fraction of their development cost. With our plans, your dream home design costs only a few hundred dollars, not the thousands of dollars that custom architects charge.

SERVICE

Once you've chosen your favorite home plan, you'll receive fast efficient service whether you choose to mail your order to us or call us toll free at 1-800-521-6797.

SATISFACTION

Our years of service to satisfied home plan buyers provide us the experience and knowledge that guarantee your satisfaction with our product and performance.

ORDER TOLL FREE 1-800-521-6797

After you've studied our Blueprint Package and Important Extras on the following pages, simply mail the accompanying order form on page 221 or call toll free on our Blueprint Hotline: 1-800-521-6797. We're ready and eager to serve you.

Each set of blueprints is an interrelated collection of floor plans, interior and exterior elevations, dimensions, cross-sections, diagrams and notations showing precisely how your house is to be constructed.

Here's what you get:

Frontal Sheet
This artist's sketch of the exterior of the house, done in realistic perspective, gives you an idea of how the house will look when built and landscaped. Large ink-line floor plans show all levels of the house and provide a quick overview of your new home's livability, as well as a handy reference for studying furniture placement.

Foundation Plan
Drawn to 1/4-inch scale, this sheet shows the complete foundation layout including support

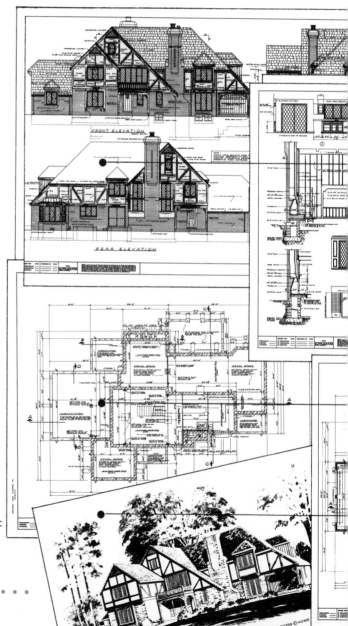

walls, excavated and unexcavated areas, if any, and foundation notes. If slab construction rather than basement, the plan shows footings and details for a monolithic slab. This page, or another in the set, also includes a sample plot plan for locating your house on a building site.

Detailed Floor Plans

Complete in 1/4-inch scale, these plans show the layout of each floor of the house. All rooms and interior spaces are carefully dimensioned and keys are provided for cross-section details given later in the plans. The positions of all electrical outlets and switches are clearly shown.

House Cross-Sections

Large-scale views, normally drawn at 3/8-inch equals 1 foot, show sections or cut-aways of the foundation, interior walls, exterior walls, floors, stairways and roof details. Additional cross-sections are given to show important changes in floor, ceiling or roof heights or the relationship of one level to another. Extremely valuable for construction, these sections show exactly how the various parts of the house fit together.

Interior Elevations

These large-scale drawings show the design and placement of kitchen and bathroom cabinets, laundry areas, fireplaces, bookcases and other built-ins. Little "extras," such as mantelpiece and wainscoting drawings, plus moulding sections, provide details that give your home that custom touch.

Exterior Elevations

Drawings in 1/4-inch scale show the front, rear and sides of your house and give necessary notes on exterior materials and finishes. Particular attention is given to cornice detail, brick and stone accents or other finish items that make your home distinctive.

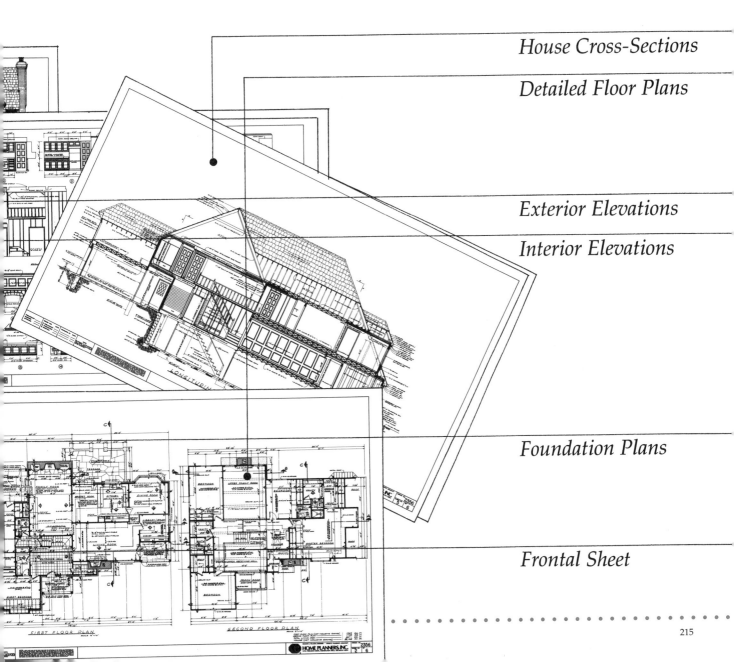

House Cross-Sections

Detailed Floor Plans

Exterior Elevations

Interior Elevations

Foundation Plans

Frontal Sheet

Important Extras To Do The Job Right!

Introducing seven important planning and construction aids developed by our professionals to help you succeed in your home-building project.

To Order, Call Toll Free 1-800-521-6797

To add these important extras to your Blueprint Package, simply indicate your choices on the order form on page 221 or call us Toll Free 1-800-521-6797 and we'll tell you more about these exciting products.

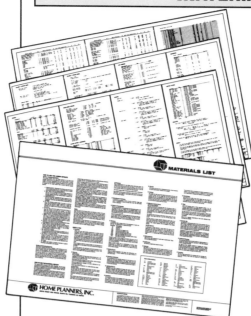

MATERIALS LIST

For many of the designs in our portfolio, we offer a customized materials take-off that is invaluable in planning and estimating the cost of your new home. This comprehensive list outlines the quantity, type and size of material needed to build your house (with the exception of mechanical system items). Included are:

- framing lumber
- roofing and sheet metal
- windows and doors
- exterior sheathing material and trim
- masonry, veneer and fireplace materials
- tile and flooring materials
- kitchen and bath cabinetry
- interior drywall and trim
- rough and finish hardware
- many more items

(Note: Because of differing local codes, building methods, and availability of materials, our Materials Lists do not include mechanical materials. To obtain necessary take-offs and recommendations, consult heating, plumbing and electrical contractors. Materials Lists are not sold separately from the Blueprint Package.)

This handy list helps you or your builder cost out materials and serves as a ready reference sheet when you're compiling bids. It also provides a cross-check against the materials specified by your builder and helps coordinate the substitution of items you may need to meet local codes.

SPECIFICATION OUTLINE

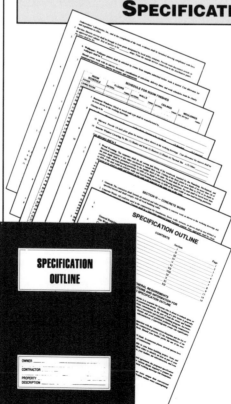

This valuable 16-page document is critical to building your house correctly. Designed to be filled in by you or your builder, this booklet lists 166 stages or items crucial to the building process.

For the layman, it provides a comprehensive review of the construction process and helps in making the specific choices of materials, models and processes. For the builder, it serves as a guide to preparing a building quotation and forms the basis for the construction program.

Designed primarily as a reference for the homeowner, this Specification Outline can become a legally binding document. Once it is filled out and agreed upon by owner and builder, it becomes a complete Project Specification.

When combined with the blueprints, a signed contract and schedule, the Specification Outline becomes a legal document and record for the building of your home. Many home builders find it useful to order two of these outlines—one as a worksheet in formulating the specifications and another to be carefully completed as a legal document.

DETAIL SHEETS

If you want to know more about techniques—and deal more confidently with subcontractors—we offer these remarkably useful detail sheets. Each is an excellent tool that will enhance your understanding of these technical subjects.

Plan-A-Home®

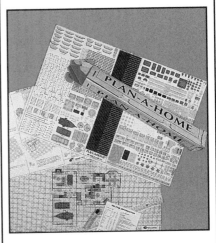

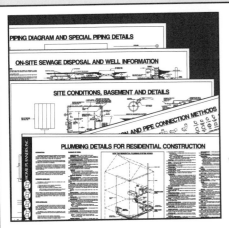

PLUMBING

The Blueprint Package includes locations for all the plumbing fixtures in your new house, including sinks, lavatories, tubs, showers, toilets, laundry trays and water heaters. However, if you want to know more about the complete plumbing system, these 24x36-inch detail sheets will prove very useful. Prepared to meet requirements of the National Plumbing Code, these six fact-filled sheets give general information on pipe schedules, fittings, sump-pump details, water-softener hookups, septic system details and much more. Color-coded sheets include a glossary of terms.

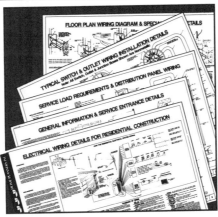

ELECTRICAL

The locations for every electrical switch, plug and outlet are shown in your Blueprint Package. However, these Electrical Details go further to take the mystery out of household electrical systems. Prepared to meet requirements of the National Electrical Code, these comprehensive 24x36-inch drawings come packed with helpful information, including wire sizing, switch-installation schematics, cable-routing details, appliance wattage, door-bell hookups, typical service panel circuitry and much more. Six sheets are bound together and color-coded for easy reference. A glossary of terms is also included.

Plan-A-Home® is an easy-to-use tool that helps you design a new home, arrange furniture in a new or existing home, or plan a remodeling project. Each package contains:

- More than *700 peel-off planning symbols* on a self-stick vinyl sheet, including walls, windows, doors, all types of furniture, kitchen components, bath fixtures and many more. All are made of durable, peel-and-stick vinyl you can use over and over.

- A reusable, transparent, *1/4-inch scale planning grid* made of tough mylar that matches the scale of actual working drawings (1/4-inch equals 1 foot). This grid provides the basis for house layouts of up to 140x92 feet.

- *Tracing paper* and a protective sheet for copying or transferring your completed plan.

- A *felt-tip pen*, with water-soluble ink that wipes away quickly.

CONSTRUCTION

The Blueprint Package contains everything an experienced builder needs to construct a particular house. However, it doesn't show all the ways that houses can be built, nor does it explain alternate construction methods. To help you understand how your house will be built—and offer additional techniques—this set of drawings depicts the materials and methods used to build foundations, fireplaces, walls, floors and roofs. Where appropriate, the drawings show acceptable alternatives. These six sheets will answer questions for the advanced do-it-yourselfer or home planner.

MECHANICAL

This package contains fundamental principles and useful data that will help you make informed decisions and communicate with subcontractors about heating and cooling systems. The 24 x 36-inch drawings contain instructions and samples that allow you to make simple load calculations and preliminary sizing and costing analysis. Covered are today's most commonly used systems from heat pumps to solar fuel systems. The package is packed full of illustrations and diagrams to help you visualize components and how they relate to one another.

With Plan-A-Home®, you can make basic planning decisions for a new house or make modifications to an existing house. Use with your Blueprint Package to test modifications to rooms or to plan furniture arrangements before you build. Plan-A-Home® lets you lay out areas as large as a 7,500 square foot, six-bedroom, seven-bath house.

House Blueprint Price Schedule and Plans Index

These pages contain all the information you need to price your blueprints. In general the larger and more complicated the house, the more it costs to design and thus the higher the price we must charge for the blueprints. Remember, however, that these prices are far less than you would normally pay for the services of a licensed architect or professional designer. Custom home designs and related architectural services often cost thousands of dollars, ranging from 5% to 15% of the cost of construction. By ordering our blueprints you are potentially saving enough money to afford a larger house, or to add those "extra" amenities such as a patio, deck, swimming pool or even an upgraded kitchen or luxurious master suite.

To use the Index below, refer to the design number listed in numerical order (a helpful page reference is also given). Note the price index letter and refer to the House Blueprint Price Schedule at right for the cost of one, four or eight sets of blueprints or the cost of a reproducible sepia. Additional prices are shown for identical and reverse blueprint sets, as well as a very useful Materials List for some of the plans.

House Blueprint Price Schedule
(Prices guaranteed through December 31, 1994)

	1-set Study Package	4-set Building Package	8-set Building Package	1-set Reproducible Sepias
Schedule A	$210	$270	$330	$420
Schedule B	$240	$300	$360	$480
Schedule C	$270	$330	$390	$540
Schedule D	$300	$360	$420	$600
Schedule E	$390	$450	$510	$660

Additional Identical Blueprints in same order ....$50 per set
Reverse Blueprints (mirror image) ....$50 per set
Specification Outlines...$7 each
Materials Lists (for Home Planners', Design Basics', Alan Mascord's, and Donald Gardner's Plans only):

▲ Home Planners' Designs...$40
† Design Basics' Designs..$75
◆ Donald Gardner's Designs $40
✷ Alan Mascord's Designs $40

Exchanges.........................$40 exchange fee for the first set; $10 for each additional set
$60 total exchange fee for 4 sets
$90 total exchange fee for 8 sets

To Order: Fill in and send the Order Form on page 221—or call us Toll Free 1-800-521-6797.

Before You Order . . .

Before completing the coupon at right or calling us on our Toll-Free Blueprint Hotline, you may be interested to learn more about our service and products. Here's some information you will find helpful.

Quick Turnaround
We process and ship every blueprint order from our office within 48 hours. On most orders, we do even better. Normally, if we receive your order by 5 p.m. Eastern Time, we'll process it the same day and ship it the following day. Because of this quick turnaround, we won't send a formal notice acknowledging receipt of your order.

Our Exchange Policy
Since blueprints are printed in response to your order, we cannot honor requests for refunds. However, we will exchange your entire first order for an equal number of blueprints plus the following exchange fees: $40 for the first set, $10 for each additional set; $60 total exchange fee for 4 sets; $90 total exchange fee for 8 sets.... *plus* the difference in cost if exchanging for a design in a higher price bracket, or *less* the difference in cost if exchanging for a design in a lower price bracket. (Sepias are not exchangeable.) All sets from the first order must be returned before the exchange can take place. Please add $8 for postage and handling via ground service; $20 via 2nd Day Air.

About Reverse Blueprints
If you want to build in reverse of the plan as shown, we will include an extra set of reversed blueprints (mirror image) for an additional fee of $50. Although lettering and dimensions appear backward, reverses will be a useful visual aid if you decide to flop the plan.

Modifying Our Plans
With such a great selection of homes, you are bound to find the one that suits you. However, if you need to make changes to the plans you have chosen, it may be easy for us to do this for you. Please ask for additional information when you place your order.

If you decide to revise plans significantly that are not customizable, we strongly suggest that you order reproducible sepias and consult a licensed architect or professional designer to help you redraw the plans.

Architectural and Engineering Seals
Some cities and states are now requiring that a licensed architect or engineer review and "seal" your blueprints prior to construction. This is often due to local or regional concerns over energy consumption, safety codes, seismic ratings, etc. For this reason, you may find it necessary to consult with a local professional to have your plans reviewed. This can normally be accomplished with minimum delays, for a nominal fee.

Compliance with Local Codes and Regulations
At the time of creation, our plans are drawn to specifications published by Building Officials Code Administrators (BOCA), the Southern Standard Building Code, or the Uniform Building Code and are designed to meet or exceed national building standards. Some states, counties and municipalities have their own codes, zoning requirements and building regulations. Before starting construction, consult with local building authorities and make sure you comply with local ordinances and codes, including obtaining any necessary permits or inspections as building progresses. In some cases, minor modifications to your plans by your builder, local architect or designer may be required to meet local conditions and requirements.

Foundation and Exterior Wall Changes
Most of our plans are drawn with either a full or partial basement foundation. Depending upon your specific climate or regional building practices, you may wish to convert this basement to a slab or crawlspace. Most professional contractors and builders can easily adapt your plans to alternate foundation types. Likewise, most can easily convert 2x4 wall construction to 2x6, or vice versa. If you need more guidance on these conversions, our handy Construction Detail Sheets, shown on page 217, describe how such conversions can be made.

How Many Blueprints Do You Need?
A single set of blueprints is sufficient to study a home in greater detail. However, if you are planning to obtain cost estimates from a contractor or subcontractors—or if you are planning to build immediately—you will need more sets. Because additional sets are cheaper when ordered in quantity with the original order, make sure you order enough blueprints to satisfy all requirements. The following checklist will help you determine how many you need:

_____Owner

_____Builder (generally requires at least three sets; one as a legal document, one to use during inspections, and at least one to give to subcontractors)

_____Local Building Department (often requires two sets)

_____Mortgage Lender (usually one set for a conventional loan; three sets for FHA or VA loans)

_____TOTAL NUMBER OF SETS

Toll Free 1-800-521-6797
Normal Office Hours:
8:00 a.m. to 8:00 p.m. Eastern Time
Monday through Friday
Our staff will gladly answer any questions during normal office hours. Our answering service can place orders after hours or on weekends.

If we receive your order by 5:00 p.m. Eastern Time, Monday through Friday, we'll process it the same day and ship it the following business day. When ordering by phone, please have your charge card ready. We'll also ask you for the Order Form Key Number at the bottom of the coupon. Please use our Toll-Free number for blueprint and book orders only.

By FAX: Copy the Order Form on the next page and send it on our International FAX line: 1-602-297-6219.

Canadian Customers
Order Toll-Free 1-800-848-2550
For faster, more economical service, Canadian customers may now call in orders on our Toll-Free line. Or, complete the order form at right, adding 30% to all prices and mail with your check in Canadian funds to:

Home Planners, Inc.
3275 W. Ina Road, Suite 110
Tucson, AZ 85741

By FAX: Copy the Order Form on the next page and send it on our International FAX line: 1-602-297-6219.

O R D E R   F O R M

**HOME PLANNERS, INC., 3275 WEST INA ROAD
SUITE 110, TUCSON, ARIZONA 85741**

E BASIC BLUEPRINT PACKAGE
sh me the following (please refer to the Plans Index and
e Schedule in this section):

____ Set(s) of blueprints for plan number(s) _____. $_____
____ Set(s) of sepias for plan number(s) _____. $_____
____ Additional identical blueprints in same order
@ $50 per set. $_____
____ Reverse blueprints @ $50 per set. $_____

PORTANT EXTRAS
sh me the following:

____ Materials List: $40 Home Planners' Designs;
$75 Design Basics' Designs; $40 Alan Mascord's
Designs; $40 Donald Gardner's Designs. $_____
____ Specification Outlines @ $7 each. $_____
____ Detail Sets @ $14.95 each; any two for $22.95; three
for $29.95; all four $39.95 (save $19.85). $_____
❑ Plumbing ❑ Electrical ❑ Construction ❑ Mechanical
(These helpful details provide general construction
advice and are not specific to any single plan.)
____ Plan-A-Home® @ $29.95 each. $_____
B-TOTAL $_____
LES TAX (Arizona residents add 5% sales tax; Michigan
residents add 4% sales tax.) $_____

POSTAGE AND ANDLING	1-3 sets	4 or more sets	
LIVERY (Requires street dress - No P.O. Boxes) egular Service llow 4-6 days delivery	❑ $6.00	❑ $8.00	$_____
nd Day Air llow 2-3 days delivery	❑ $12.00	❑ $20.00	$_____
ext Day Air llow 1 day delivery	❑ $22.00	❑ $30.00	$_____
ST OFFICE DELIVERY no street address available. low 4-6 days delivery	❑ $8.00	❑ $12.00	$_____
VERSEAS AIR MAIL LIVERY te: All delivery times are from e Blueprint Package is shipped.	❑ $30.00	❑ $50.00	$_____
	❑ Send COD		

TAL (Sub-total, tax, and postage) $_____

UR ADDRESS (please print)

ame _____
reet _____
ty _____ State _____ Zip _____
aytime telephone number (_____) _____

R CREDIT CARD ORDERS ONLY
ease fill in the information below:

edit card number _____
xp. Date: Month/Year_____
heck one ❑ Visa ❑ MasterCard ❑ Discover Card

gnature _____

rder Form Key Please check appropriate box:
❑ Licensed Builder-Contractor
❑ Home Owner

[TB31BP]

☎ **ORDER TOLL FREE
1-800-521-6797**

O R D E R   F O R M

**HOME PLANNERS, INC., 3275 WEST INA ROAD
SUITE 110, TUCSON, ARIZONA 85741**

THE BASIC BLUEPRINT PACKAGE
Rush me the following (please refer to the Plans Index and
Price Schedule in this section):

____ Set(s) of blueprints for plan number(s) _____. $_____
____ Set(s) of sepias for plan number(s) _____. $_____
____ Additional identical blueprints in same order
@ $50 per set. $_____
____ Reverse blueprints @ $50 per set. $_____

IMPORTANT EXTRAS
Rush me the following:

____ Materials List: $40 Home Planners' Designs;
$75 Design Basics' Designs; $40 Alan Mascord's
Designs; $40 Donald Gardner's Designs. $_____
____ Specification Outlines @ $7 each. $_____
____ Detail Sets @ $14.95 each; any two for $22.95; three
for $29.95; all four $39.95 (save $19.85). $_____
❑ Plumbing ❑ Electrical ❑ Construction ❑ Mechanical
(These helpful details provide general construction
advice and are not specific to any single plan.)
____ Plan-A-Home® @ $29.95 each. $_____
SUB-TOTAL $_____
SALES TAX (Arizona residents add 5% sales tax; Michigan
residents add 4% sales tax.) $_____

POSTAGE AND HANDLING	1-3 sets	4 or more sets	
DELIVERY (Requires street address - No P.O. Boxes) •Regular Service Allow 4-6 days delivery	❑ $6.00	❑ $8.00	$_____
•2nd Day Air Allow 2-3 days delivery	❑ $12.00	❑ $20.00	$_____
•Next Day Air Allow 1 day delivery	❑ $22.00	❑ $30.00	$_____
POST OFFICE DELIVERY If no street address available. Allow 4-6 days delivery	❑ $8.00	❑ $12.00	$_____
OVERSEAS AIR MAIL DELIVERY Note: All delivery times are from date Blueprint Package is shipped.	❑ $30.00	❑ $50.00	$_____
	❑ Send COD		

TOTAL (Sub-total, tax, and postage) $_____

YOUR ADDRESS (please print)

Name _____
Street _____
City _____ State _____ Zip _____
Daytime telephone number (_____) _____

FOR CREDIT CARD ORDERS ONLY
Please fill in the information below:

Credit card number _____
Exp. Date: Month/Year_____
Check one ❑ Visa ❑ MasterCard ❑ Discover Card

Signature _____

Order Form Key Please check appropriate box:
❑ Licensed Builder-Contractor
❑ Home Owner

[TB31BP]

☎ **ORDER TOLL FREE
1-800-521-6797**

Additional Plans Books

THE DESIGN CATEGORY SERIES

1.

ONE-STORY HOMES
A collection of 470 homes to suit a range of budgets in one-story living. All popular styles, including Cape Cod, Southwestern, Tudor and French. **384 pages. $8.95 ($11.95 Canada)**

2.

TWO-STORY HOMES
478 plans for all budgets in a wealth of styles: Tudors, Salt-boxes, Farmhouses, Victorians, Georgians, Contemporaries and more. **416 pages. $8.95 ($11.95 Canada)**

3.

MULTI-LEVEL AND HILL-SIDE HOMES 312 distinctive styles for both flat and sloping sites. Includes exposed lower levels, open staircases, balconies, decks and terraces. **320 pages. $6.95 ($9.95 Canada)**

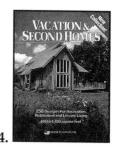

4.

VACATION AND SECOND HOMES 258 ideal plans for a favorite vacation spot or perfect retirement or starter home. Includes cottages, chalets, and 1-, 1½-, 2-, and multi-levels. **256 pages. $5.95 ($7.95 Canada)**

THE EXTERIOR STYLE SERIES

9.

THE ESSENTIAL GUIDE TO TRADITIONAL HOMES
Over 400 traditional homes in one special volume. American and European styles from Farmhouses to Norman French. "Readers' Choice" highlights best sellers in four-color photographs and renderings. **304 pages. $9.95 U.S. ($12.95 Canada)**

10.

THE ESSENTIAL GUIDE TO CONTEMPORARY HOMES More than 340 contemporary designs from Northwest Contemporary to Post-Modern Victorian. Four-color section of best sellers; two-color illustrations and line drawings throughout the remainder. **304 pages. $9.95 U.S. ($12.95 Canada)**

11.

VICTORIAN DREAM HOMES 160 Victorian and Farmhouse designs by three master designers. Victorian style from Second Empire homes through the Queen Anne and Folk Victorian era. Beautifully drawn renderings accompany the modern floor plans. **192 pages. $12.95 ($16.95 Canada)**

12.

WESTERN HOME PLANS
Over 215 home plans from Spanish Mission and Monter to Northwest Chateau and Sa Francisco Victorian. Historic notes trace the background and geographical incidence c each style. **208 pages. $8.95 ($11.95 Canada)**

OUR BEST PLAN PORTFOLIOS

NEW ENCYCLOPEDIA OF HOME DESIGNS
Our best collection of plans is now bigger and better than ever! Over 500 plans organized by architectural category including all types and styles and 269 brand-new plans. The most comprehensive plan book ever.

15. **352 pages. $9.95 ($12.95 Canada)**

AFFORDABLE HOME PLANS For the prospective home builder with a modest or medium budget. Features 430 one-, 1½-, two-story and multi-level homes in a wealth of styles. Included are cost saving ideas for the budget-conscious.

16. **320 pages. $8.95 ($11.95 Canada)**

LUXURY DREAM HOMES At last, the home you've waited f A collection of 150 of best luxury home pla from seven of the mos highly regarded desig ers and architects in t United States. A drea come true for anyone interested in designin building or remodelin luxury home.

17. **192 pages. $14.95 ($17.95 Canada)**

HOME IMPROVEMENT AND LANDSCAPE BOOKS

5.

THE HOME REMODELER
A revolutionary book of 31 remodeling plans backed by complete construction-ready blueprints and materials lists. Sections on kitchens, baths, master bedrooms and much more. Ideas galore; helpful advice and valuable suggestions. **112 pages. $7.95 U.S. ($10.95 Canada)**

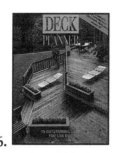

6.

DECK PLANNER 25 practical plans and details for decks the do-it-yourselfer can actually build. How-to data and project starters for a variety of decks. Construction details available separately. **112 pages. $7.95 ($10.95 Canada)**

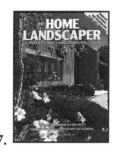

7.

THE HOME LANDSCAPER
55 fabulous front and back-yard plans that even the do-it-youselfer can master. Complete construction blueprints and regionalized plant lists available for each design. **208 pages. $12.95 ($16.95 Canada)**

8.

BACKYARD LANDSCAPER
Sequel to the popular *Home Landscaper*, contains 40 professionally designed plans for backyards to do yourself or contract out. Complete construction blueprints and regionalized plant lists available. **160 pages. $12.95 ($16.95 Canada)**

INTRODUCING THE NEW BLUE RIBBON DESIGNER SERIES

13.

200 FARMHOUSES & COUNTRY HOME PLANS Styles and sizes to match every taste and budget. Grouped by type, the homes represent a variety from Classic Farmhouses to Country Capes & Cottages. Introductions and expertly drawn floor plans and renderings enhance the sections. **224 pages. $6.95 ($9.95 Canada)**

14.

200 BUDGET-SMART HOME PLANS The definitive source for the home builder with a limited budget, this volume shows that you can have your home and enjoy it, too! Amenity-laden homes, in many sizes and styles, can all be built from our plans. **224 pages. $6.95 ($9.95 Canada)**

Please fill out the coupon below. We will process your order and ship it from our office within 48 hours. Send coupon and check for the total to:

HOME PLANNERS, INC.
3275 West Ina Road, Suite 110, Dept. BK
Tucson, Arizona 85741

THE DESIGN CATEGORY SERIES—A great series of books edited by design type. Complete collection features 1376 pages and 1273 home plans.

1. _____ One-Story Homes @ $8.95 ($11.95 Canada) $ _____
2. _____ Two-Story Homes @ $8.95 ($11.95 Canada) $ _____
3. _____ Multi-Level & Hillside Homes @ $6.95 ($9.95 Canada) $ _____
4. _____ Vacation & Second Homes @ $5.95 ($7.95 Canada) $ _____

HOME IMPROVEMENT AND LANDSCAPE BOOKS

5. _____ The Home Remodeler @ $7.95 ($10.95 Canada) $ _____
6. _____ Deck Planner @ $7.95 ($10.95 Canada) $ _____
7. _____ The Home Landscaper @ $12.95 ($16.95 Canada) $ _____
8. _____ The Backyard Landscaper @ $12.95 ($16.95 Canada) $ _____

THE EXTERIOR STYLE SERIES

9. _____ Traditional Homes Plans @ $9.95 ($12.95 Canada) $ _____
10. _____ Contemporary Homes Plans @ $9.95 ($12.95 Canada) $ _____
11. _____ Victorian Dream Homes @ $12.95 ($16.95 Canada) $ _____
12. _____ Western Home Plans @ $8.95 ($11.95 Canada) $ _____

THE BLUE RIBBON DESIGNER SERIES

13. _____ 200 Farmhouse & Country Home Plans @ $6.95 ($9.95 Canada) $ _____
14. _____ 200 Budget-Smart Home Plans @ $6.95 ($9.95 Canada) $ _____

OUR BEST PLAN PORTFOLIOS

15. _____ New Encyclopedia of Home Designs @ $9.95 ($12.95 Canada) $ _____
16. _____ Affordable Home Plans @ $8.95 ($11.95 Canada) $ _____
17. _____ Luxury Dream Homes @ $14.95 ($17.95 Canada) $ _____

Sub-Total $ _____
Arizona residents add 5% sales tax; Michigan residents add 4% sales tax $ _____
ADD Postage and Handling $ _____
TOTAL (Please enclose check) $ 3.00

Name (please print) _____
Address _____
City _____ State _____ Zip _____

CANADIAN CUSTOMERS: Order books Toll-Free 1-800-848-2550. Or, complete the order form above, using Canadian prices, and mail with your check in Canadian funds to: Home Planners, Inc. 3275 W. Ina Road, Suite 110, Tucson, AZ 85741.

 TO ORDER BOOKS BY PHONE CALL TOLL FREE 1-800-322-6797

TB31BK

OVER 3 MILLION BLUEPRINTS SOLD

"We instructed our builder to follow the plans including all of the many details which make this house so elegant... Our home is a fine example of the results one can achieve by purchasing and following the plans which you offer... Everyone who has seen it has assured us that it belongs in 'a picture book.' I truly mean it when I say that my home 'is a DREAM HOUSE.'"

S.P.
Anderson, SC

"We have had a steady stream of visitors, many of whom tell us this is the most beautiful home they've seen. Everyone is amazed at the layout and remark on how unique it is. Our real estate attorney, who is a Chicago dweller and who deals with highly valued properties, told me this is the only suburban home he has seen that he would want to live in."

W. & P.S.
Flossmoor, IL

"Home Planners' blueprints saved us a great deal of money. I acted as the general contractor and we did a lot of the work ourselves. We probably built it for half the cost! We are thinking about more plans for another home. I purchased a competitor's book but my husband only wants your plans!"

K.M.
Grovetown, GA

"We are very happy with the product of our efforts. The neighbors and passersby appreciate what we have created. We have had many people stop by to discuss our house and kindly praise it as being the nicest house in our area of new construction. We have even had one person stop and make us an unsolicited offer to buy the house for much more than we have invested in it."

K. & L.S.
Bolingbrook, IL

"The traffic going past our house is unbelievable. On several occasions, we have heard that it is the 'prettiest house in Batavia.' Also, when meeting someone new and mentioning what street we live on, quite often we're told, 'Oh, you're the one in the yellow house with the wrap-around porch! I love it!'"

A.W.
Batavia, NY

"I have been involved in the building trades my entire life... Since building our home we have built two other homes for other families. Their plans from local professional architects were not nearly as good as yours. For that reason we are ordering additional plan books from you."

T.F.
Kingston, WA

"The blueprints we received from Home Planners were of excellent quality and provided us with exactly what we needed to get our successful home-building project underway. We appreciate Home Planners' invaluable role in our home-building effort."

T.A.
Concord, TN